ENDORSEMENTS

"I swear, this book was written with my wife in mind. Okay, not really, but it could have been. It's brilliant, poetic, raw, real, vulnerable, and everything the Christian faith should be but isn't. It almost reads as a journal of sorts, where the author lets her readers take a look at what's going on in her head. This takes guts, and I applaud Shock for taking such a risk (and pulling it off!!!). Recommended reading for anyone who has wrestled with their faith."

— **Matthew J. Distefano**, author of *The Wisdom of Hobbits*, producer of the Heretic Happy Hour podcast, and columnist for *Patheos*

"This book has captured the heart of a life's journey. Karen has picked the choices pieces of life and contained them in a book that calls to the heart of every human being. Karen has embodied the raw, organic, heart cry of every person who has suffered through fundamental religion. A religion that focuses on performance over the person. You will cry, shout and shake your head in agreement as she takes you through the pains of discovering that life is to be lived fully free not just the drudgery of compliant rules. As a poet I love the rhythm of her writing as it carries the reader on the winds of exploration. You will not be disappointed in reading this marvelous book of life."

— **Roger Barnett**, co-host of SQ1, poet, writer

"*In Too Much and Not Enough*, author Karen Shock vulnerably shares her journey to uncover her authentic self while questioning the very foundation on which her life was built—her faith. This powerful, poignant collection of poems will change lives for the better, especially those who love God but question their place in the church."

— **Kiersten Hathcock**, author of *Little Voices*, and Co-Founder of National Institute for Law and Justice

"Courageously and authentically, my friend Karen Shock leads the reader through a delightful journey in Jesus...minus all of the legalism and rules. She lays out her life journey and tells her own story in a very unique and easy-to-read style. You will not be able to put this book down and when you finish it, her stories will stay with you as they are very relatable."

— **Todd R. Vick**, author of *The Renewing of Your Mind* and *The Reconstructing of Your Mind*

"It is a rare work of art that can help us find beauty within the brokenness of our own story. In *Too Much and Not Enough* Karen Shock does exactly that. Her transparency is breathtaking and fills our souls with hope that we too can navigate a twisted road to a happy ending. This book is pure poetry magic and I loved every second of reading it."

— **Jason Elam**, co-host of *The Messy Spirituality Podcast*

"So many 'oh yes me too' moments as I read this. The honesty of Karen's writing is so validating for all of us on this journey of seeking and learning and re-creating. Short and intentional chapters ensure that even those of us with little ones clamoring all over us are still able to read and receive this wisdom. Don't miss this one!"

— **Elizabeth Enns Petters**, co-host of the *Deconstructing Mamas* Podcast, contributing author to *Deconstructing Hell*

"Karen hasn't written a book as much as she's created a companion for your journey. *Too Much and Not Enough* will be a book that you come back to again and again as you come across experiences in your life that grow, evolve, and shift your faith in the Divine. If your heart and mind are filled with changing thoughts about life and faith and what it all means ... Karen will help you put words on those feelings and be a peace with them. Do yourself a favor and add this book to your collection!"

— **Dr. Glenn Siepert**, host of the *What If Project* Podcast and author of *(Re)Thinking Everything*

"Karen's writing feels like a hug from a wise but perfectly imperfect big sister. Her whimsical and humor-filled style present deep and profound self-observations while simultaneously bringing a lightness to even the heaviest of subject matter. Through honest and playful storytelling, Shock invites readers to reflect upon their own lives from a place of curiosity about life's big and little questions. Questions about faith, family, mental health, pain, loss, love and more. She reminds us that the human experience with all of its struggle and strife, can be an ever-evolving gift."

— **Margot Harris and Abigail Wilber**, co-hosts of *The Anxiety Warriors Podcast*

"In my opinion poetry is one of the best ways to open your heart and invite others along for the journey. Karen Shock has done this with her new book *Too Much and Not Enough*. The book is a mix of memoir and poetry. Karen asks us to join her in a place that allows for doubting, questioning and searching. Her poetry is at the same time raw and beautiful, timely and timeless, heartbreaking and hopeful. Are you someone that has found themselves ok with the hard questions? Are you someone willing to lose your faith to find one that is better? Then, this book is for you."

— **Jon Turney**, co-host of *This Is Not Church* Podcast

"Stepping into this book is like being invited into Karen's life. As you read, you can feel with her heart, see with her eyes, and think with her mind. This book is real. Maybe too real for some. And maybe that's the point. Karen brings you along her own journey beyond the conditioning and certainty of religion, while still inviting you to know a Jesus who transcends our beliefs, tribes, and churches with an ever- present embrace of everything. So good."

— **Kevin Sweeney**, author of *The Making of Mystic* and *The Joy of Letting Go*

"I'm not necessarily one for poetry, but I found myself absolutely inspired by Karen's vulnerability and 'Amen-ing' to so much of what she shared. It was as if she openly invited me into her life to connect with an authentic human being. *Too Much and Not Enough* is an honest, welcoming, and poetic reminder that even though all of us at times may feel too much and not enough, we are truly never too much and always enough. No matter where you are in your deconstruction journey, you will find healing in this book."

— **Justin Tang**, Religious Trauma Coach

"Organized religion is a tough spot for authentic people. Karen gave her heart and soul over and over again, but found it hard to fit in because she was evolving and growing. Too much for one group, not enough for another. But she did the right thing. Instead of becoming small, she got bigger and eventually didn't apologize for it. Then she wrote her story poetically and started to share it with those that deserved to hear it. Deconstruction is hard, but ultimately, living small is harder. We honor her for having the courage to be brave and vulnerable and lean into her trauma."

— **Karl and Laura Forehand**, Authors of *Out Into the Desert* and founders of *The Desert Sanctuary*

"In *Too Much and Not Enough*, Karen Ruth Shock speaks poetry into the messiness and beauty of life. In looking at her own life through a deep and discerning lens, Karen connects us all through shared humanity. By revealing her joys and struggles and breaking them down to their cores, Karen gently nudges us into our own self-examination as we all grapple with what it means to be human. Karen reminds us that when we ask the hard questions, we grow...even when the answers are nonexistent or unexpected. Raw, honest, transparent, unfiltered, Too Much and Not Enough is ultimately a book of optimism and hope. Karen Ruth Shock lets us know that the journey to self-acceptance is ongoing, and that is OK."

— **Abbey Hoffman**, M.Ed, wife, mom, teacher

"*Too Much and Not Enough* isn't just a book about Karen's life. It's an invitation to transparency and authentic inner dialogue we've all been craving. It's all the things we thought but dared not say and some we were too afraid to think. It's for those of us who have tried so hard—for *so* long—to walk the straight and narrow of our faith only to find we never really felt like we had it all together or that we were able to do all the things, all the time, for all the people. Karen shares about traumas people of faith are often encouraged to bypass. She addresses struggles we've not been able to openly share and her journey of self-advocacy. Reading this book will not only give you a feeling of belonging, but it will show you just how normal it is to question, especially in the midst of hard experiences. It invites you into a space where you can be you and it really is completely ok. It's one of the most incredible personable reading experiences I've had. You'll walk away from this book feeling as if Karen is one of your oldest and dearest friends."

— **Joann McAfee Maldonado**, Humanity Advocate, Anti-Racist, Lover of All

"I have come to realize that truth has a cadence...a distinct and recognizable rhythm. From the first line to the last, Karen Ruth Shock draws us into the eb and flow of faith... the inevitable dissonance between doctrine and decision. *Too Much and Not Enough* is both a teacher and a pupil, a leader and a follower, a destination and a journey. We get to see through the eyes of Shock into ourselves and therefore into the heart of God... a God who is big enough for every single one of us. And though she wades into the deep, Shock keeps us afloat by flouting the rules of literary restraint with delightful intention... showing us in Too Much and Not Enough that pain can be poetry, and serenity can be the song that dares us to find freedom, inviting us toward the light, helping us to live loved."

— **Desimber Rose**, poet, spoken word artist, author of *The Church Can Go to Hell*

"I felt like I was reading my own thoughts. It was like weighted blanket making you feel warm and held. Not alone. Knowing that other people have these same intrusive or reserved thoughts as I do. It really pulled me in which is hard to do, I only want to read something if I feel like it is going to help me grow and apply the tools I learn into my life. This book did just that."

— **Anna Miller**, Professional Dancer

"Karen's vulnerability in *Too Much and Not Enough* is both refreshing and inspiring. Her unique writing style and unbridled honesty pulled me in right away, and her words made me feel seen. This book is truly unique and compelling, and I know it will be vastly impactful for anyone who's experienced brokenness in their faith journey!"

— **Jonah Baker**, Musical Artist, YouTuber

TOO MUCH AND NOT ENOUGH

SACRED THOUGHTS SAID OUT LOUD

KAREN SHOCK

All rights reserved. No part of this book may be used or reproduced, stored in a retrieval system, or transmitted in any form or by any means, electronic, mechanical, photocopying, recording, scanning, or otherwise, without written permission from the publisher except in the case of brief quotations embodied in critical articles and reviews. Permission for wider usage of this material can be obtained through Quoir by emailing permission@quoir.com.

Copyright © 2023 by Karen Shock, First Edition

Cover Design by Rafael Polendo (polendo.net)
Interior Layout by Matthew J. Distefano

ISBN 978-1-957007-64-9

Printed in the United States of America

QUOIR

Published by Quoir
Chico, California
www.quoir.com

~ For Kev ~
Is this real?
Did we really do this?
A real book?
Team Shock.
These pages are filled with our story.
And you are the hero in so much of it.
Thank you for being my best friend.
I love you.
&
I love our story.

CONTENTS

FOREWORD	XV
PREFACE	XIX
PART I	1
misfit	2
who am i?	7
i'm thinking about it	10
cute	12
how would i explain my anxiety?	16
a love story	19
c-section	25
how did i become brave?	29
from one brave momma to another	33
who am i to judge	36
just a kid	41
a good home	43
PART II	47
journals for days	48

dramatically reasonable	51
the shame of it all	54
purity	58
an apology (from a true love waits leader)	62
we gave grace...and then took it away	66
i was told not to trust myself	69
i used my depravity as an excuse	75
let's not grovel	80
PART III	83
loved and accepted	84
being a lifelong learner	87
freedom to be different	90
when this happens...then	94
defining moments: encouragement for the weary mom	97
the struggle is real	102
we need each other	105
no strings attached?	108
don't be confused, karen	111
PART IV	117
be still and know	118
perspective	120
values	121
is this real?	125

i'm an orphan	129
the faith of my parents	132
rapture ptsd	136
conspiracy theories	140
PART V	145
the need for certainty	146
was my anxiety a demon?	152
stay in the ranks	157
belonging	161
toxic	165
i can't unsee all i've seen	170
willing to listen	175
i lost my voice	179
PART VI	185
yellow	186
s'up	188
i'm not leaving the faith	191
we're in this race together	194
power	197
a messy, muddy life	200
in the midnight hour	204
an open heart	208
leave the light on	213

grown up kids	216
easy like sunday morning	220
i can feel it in the air	226
team up	229
grateful	232
full of delight	235
there's no ending, karen	239
THANKS	243

FOREWORD

Two things can be true at the same time, even when you feel like they're opposites. This is something I tell my clients constantly.

Hi, my name is Laci Bean and I'm a certified Trauma Recovery Coach whose focus is Religious Trauma.

You may know me from Tik Tok, @Laci_Bean. Yeah, that girl, the one with the purple hair.

My work in trauma recovery is with those who are deconstructing their faith. A process in which someone decides to re-examine and unpack their long held religious beliefs.

Well, I've been slowly deconstructing for the better part of 10 years but didn't realize it till the world came crashing down in 2020 and my deconstruction journey took a hard nosedive right off the side of a cliff.

It was hard, lonely, heartbreaking, and yet liberating at the same time. So badly I wanted to rewind time and go back to being my blissfully ignorant conservative Christian self. But, on the other hand I was enjoying the journey of thinking, feeling, and learning on my own terms.

It may have been scary but for once I felt like I was finally finding my authentic self and I loved her… deeply. I wouldn't—no actually I couldn't—give her up.

You mean, just pretend that I hadn't seen, heard, and learned everything I had for the past few months? Umm, no, that's impossible.

So, I decided to embrace this wild journey with no inkling on where it was taking me, but I didn't stop there. I took it one step further—ok maybe 20,000 steps further—and I decided to share my journey in real time with the world through Tik Tok.

It is through our own personal journeys of deconstruction and stepping out to share it with the world that Karen and I crossed paths.

When it comes to deconstruction it's something that you don't understand unless you've walked it yourself. So, when you meet a fellow traveler on this journey you instantly bond. Maybe it's because we're still healing from the loss of community when we left church, and our hearts just so desperately want that feeling of comradery again or maybe it's our shared traumas and life experiences that bond us.

Whatever the reason is, I'm here for it because I love making friends and Karen has become just that. Have we met in person yet? Actually no, but this wild journey of questioning your beliefs knows no bounds. With the beauty of social media it has allowed many of us to connect and develop deep and meaningful relationships despite living in different time zones.

Not only do Karen and I share the common bond of deconstructing our faith, but we also share many commonalities when it comes to our personalities; bubbly, loud, energetic and we both have the wonderful gift of having ADHD. I myself, consider it to be a superpower. Can you think about 13 things at the same time while simultaneously forgetting why you walked into a room? No? Okay then. Superpower.

Anyway, enough about us, let's talk about this book.

For many of us our time in church was spent hiding the parts of us that didn't fit in the pretty "Christian box" we were handed when we walked through those church doors.

Questions about the faith? Hide it.

Doubts or confusion? Hide it.

Disagreements? Hide it.

Just fit in this box and you'll be accepted and loved.

But when it's all said and done we just spend years sacrificing ourselves for the sake of fitting in; when in reality we were born to be our uniquely awkward and beautiful selves, flaws and all.

Throughout this book, Karen exposes all the parts we spent our lives hiding in a way that helps you transform them into something you're proud of.

Page after page you will see yourself in her writings and in her life story, making you feel seen, heard, and loved. Then, before you know it your shame and guilt will start melting away.

Her vulnerability and passion seep from every page in her beautiful and unique writing style that my ADHD brain *loves*.

Deconstruction isn't easy but there's beauty and freedom in the reconstruction process. Karen's book is a beacon of hope for those who desire to reconstruct their beliefs with love, hope, and authenticity at the center. Through her writing she shows how reconstruction is not only possible but liberating.

So, if you're deconstructing in any way, trying to find hope and guidance in the reconstruction of your faith, or if you feel like you've been wearing a mask and hiding your true self during your time in church, then this book is for you.

It's going to make you cry and laugh while also bringing you joy and comfort in ways you didn't know your soul needed.

Enjoy!

— **Laci Bean**, TikTok influencer and Trauma Recovery Coach

PREFACE

Dear Reader,

We are about to embark on a journey together. I will be sharing with you some of my deepest longings, craziest fears, and biggest questions.

Before putting this book together, I thought long and hard about the consequences of you all knowing me so well. Kevin (my husband) and I discussed all of the possible outcomes at length. What people will think, what some will say, and how my vulnerability will be received. Will this be worth it in the end? Will my fragile little soul be able to handle it all?

The answer to all of these was "Yes."

I mean, here we are, right?

So, before we get started, I think it's important to fill you in a little on how we have come to this point, hoping it will help you understand the pages that follow.

I was born in the small town of Defiance, Ohio, the youngest of five. My family got "saved" at a Bill Glass Crusade before I was old enough to know what it all meant. I spent my young years learning about God and "asked him into my heart" when I was five.

I loved Jesus and believed he loved me. At least until I was nine. This is when I was introduced to Rapture Theology by a horror flick that my little eyes should have never seen. The fear of a Monster God took hold of me.

So, I lived in two different realities for most of my life... the one where God loved me, and the one where I was probably going to get my head chopped off for not loving him enough.

In high school, I still loved Jesus but I think I loved boys just as much. I knew the rules about who to date and how to keep my pants zipped up, but I broke them both.

Oops.

This got me pregnant by the time I was twenty. Not married and pregnant. Shame covered me like a dark cloud. There were rumblings around our little town about me and my ever-expanding belly.

I would eventually marry Kevin, the father of our child. We had three more children and actually became youth leaders at our church.

Eventually, we began to speak at True Love Waits events. We told those kiddos not to do what we had done. The old "don't be like us even though it worked out for us" routine.

As the years went on, I dove deeper into my faith. There were so many books to read, podcasts to listen to, and conferences to attend. And the deeper I went, the more confused I became.

I've always had questions about God. Big ones. Ones that no one wanted me to have. They still don't. I'm dangerous. My questions are dangerous. A dangerous mother of four. A youth and college leader who has become a little too dangerous to lead. Not quite your gentle and quiet spirit type of woman. My mouth got me in trouble. My questions were too much.

So, anxiety and depression set in along with the guilt and shame. Not just one cloud anymore, but a whole storm was brewing on the inside. And the more I tried to out run the storm, the more clouds appeared. I learned to hide under tables, literally. I would crawl under a table when the weight of my anxiety seemed too much to bear.

About ten years ago, I read Rob Bell's book ***Love Wins*** and I realized something. I wasn't the only one. There were others who loved God and had questions just like me. Is Hell really real? Does God choose some and not others? Why did he even create us? Is there even a God? Is the Bible inerrant? And on and on and on.

The internet helped me see there were more people like me out there. I started to ask the questions out loud...well, write them. And others said "Thank you."

So, I wrote more.

It's now 2022, and I have retired from being a homeschool mom, a substitute teacher, and a cheer coach. Also, our ten year season of taking care of my elderly parents has come to an end. Kevin and I have raised four fantastic children. Three of them are married, and their spouses fit perfectly into our little family. Our oldest daughter has four beautiful children of her own. Oh, and we have one puppy and two grand-puppies. We live in Fort Wayne, Indiana, and love it here.

I'm honestly hoping to find even more people who are on this journey with me. Others who need to know it's ok to ask questions that may not even have answers. Other wanderers who are willing to dig deep and go to the hard places. Maybe we can walk this journey together? Learn from each other? And point each other to a God that is bigger and more loving than we could ever imagine.

PART I

misfit

Too much.
Not enough.
Too old.
Too young.
Always there.
Never belonging.

Walking into a room,
longing to be seen.
Seen for who I am.

Yes.
Seen and loved for who I am.

Except?
Who really knows me?
I don't even know if I know me.

I think it all began when I was little.

In elementary school.
I remember being tossed back and forth
between the "gifted" reading group
and the "regular" reading group.

Where did I belong?
The teachers couldn't figure it out.
I certainly didn't know.

Then there's this whole personality thing.
I'm an extrovert.
Except when I'm not.

I am pretty joyful.
Except when I am ridden with anxiety.

I like being with people.
Except when I get into a public place
and wanna hide.

I write about my struggles.
I write the most when I am down.
There is healing in it.

So, people feel sorry for me.
They just wanna tell me I will be ok.

Then they see me in person and I look so normal.

I thought you had anxiety?

Then when the people who know me in real life
read one of my writings?
They are just as confused.

I would have never guessed you have anxiety!

I trust God for so many big things.
But I have a hard time with the little stuff.

One minute I really care what people think.
The next minute, I couldn't care less.

Cheer coach?
Wait, I don't know enough about stunting.

Teacher?
Nope, I'm only a sub.

Homeschool mom,
who let my kids watch Disney.

Taught True Love Waits.
Didn't wait.

Too serious about God
for my classmates in school.
Not serious enough about God
for Christians.

Trying to be pretty
when I am really just "cute."

Too liberal for conservatives.
Too conservative for liberals.
Too young to be a grandma.
Too young to take care of my parents.
Too young to fear death.

I love Jesus.
I don't feel like I fit in with his people.

I have questions.
I don't think he's mad at me for it.

I do think I am judged pretty harshly
by some of his people for these questions.

Maybe that is why I have a heart for fellow misfits.
Maybe that's why I can be so easy to talk to?

I understand that there are a whole lot of misfits.
A whole land of them maybe?

I believe Jesus lived and died for us misfits.
There is where my hope lies.
In the land of the beloved misfits.

And here's what I'm learning to do about it ~

I'm learning to be "me."
Relax into "me."

Because, honestly?
Who really does fit?
And fit into what exactly?

Maybe, just maybe...
We are all a bunch of "misfits."
Believing the lie.
Deceived into thinking we must conform.

Do we all need to be the same?
Oh man, when I think of it?

How boring.
How redundant.
How awful.

Different is good.
Being comfortable with being different is hard.

What if we could be?
Comfortable.
Content with who God made each of us to be.
Honest about who we are.

Real.

Genuine.
I've got an idea.

For today,
I'll be me.
You can be you.

I'll be comfortable with who I am.

And...

You be comfortable with who you are.

Together.

All of us.
All the "misfitness."
All the messiness.
All the different.
All together.

Learning to love.
Leaning in.

You and me.
We need each other.

who am i?

No, really.
Who am I to write a book?
To write the way I do?
How did I even come up with this style?
Why do I even think I have something worth reading?

Most of the time... I don't.

So many times I have severe post-writing syndrome,
wondering why I said all I said.

What was I thinking,
putting my thoughts out there?

What must people think of me,
my heart all out there on my sleeve?

Raw emotions.
Tender feelings.
Just simply working through it.
Yes.
Working through it for all to see.

Why?
What for?

Hmmm...
I think it's for the ones who can relate.

People tell me I'm brave.
Others probably just think I'm stupid.
Some may think I'm crazy.

I don't feel brave.
I sometimes feel stupid.
And I know I feel crazy.

I have walked through some dark nights of the soul.
I've sat under tables to feel some sort of stability over me.
Cried in the closet?
On occasion.

I've been on my knees in our bathroom.
Crying out to a God,
I'm not even sure I believed in.
Asking for help to believe.
Eyes to see.
Ears to hear.
And a soft heart.

This is how people will see Jesus in me.

It won't be by my ability to talk about God.
Or by my perfection.
Or because my outsides are all tidy.
And definitely not by how I judge my neighbor.

But...
By my love.

I'm leaning into this truth.
I am free to talk about weaknesses.
I might even boast in them.

Knowing full well,

You knowing all about me?
Well, it's ok...
As long as I love.

You knowing my struggles?
It's ok...
As long as I love.

You knowing my fears and my failures?
It's really ok...
As long as I love.

This is how I know it is ok for me to keep writing,
letting you all know you are not alone.
We have each other.

It's ok to not be ok...
As long as we love.

i'm thinking about it

A friend told me he loved reading my writing.
I walked away wondering why.
I always wonder why.

Why would anyone want to read my thoughts?
That's all they are.

Random,
sometimes silly,
thoughts.

So, I did what I do best.
I went back up later that evening and asked him.

Ummm... exactly why do you like my writing?

He smiled,
thought for a moment,
and then gave me this quote by Socrates...

~ *The unexamined life is not worth living* ~

I thought for a long time about it.
I told Kevin about it.
I told my counselor about it.
I may or may not have told my dog about it.

Because, it just makes sense.
This is what I do.
I think.
A whole lot.

Which turns into examining.
Asking the hard questions.
Looking for the answers.
Searching for the meaning.

Kev said I would make a good philosopher.
I'm thinking about it.

cute

I know, I know,
I keep going back to this word.

It's because I truly have a love/hate relationship with it.
There was a time when it was all hate.

People would say I was "cute."
My hair was "cute."
My outfits were "cute."

And I would roll my eyes.
Wait... not out loud.
I would never roll them for someone to see.
Inside.
Always rolling my eyes on the inside.
Because it wouldn't be "cute" to do it on the outside.

At some point, through the years...
I decided to embrace "cute."
I was never going to be pretty or gorgeous or beautiful.
Cute was just who I was.

I began to like being called cute.
Our house was cute.
My puppy was cute.

You're so cute, Karen.
Yep, that's me.

And I would much rather be a "Cute Karen"
than just a "Karen."
Am I right?

But sometimes that word just doesn't match up.
It isn't because I want to be a super model.
Nope.
It's deeper than all of that.

It has to do with my insides.

I really do love to have fun.

Lots of fun.
And fun can be cute.
I also have some depth though.
A depth in me that isn't necessarily of the "cute" variety.
A depth of the "deep" variety.

And when I go deep,
it's not always fun.

My brain spirals.
My thoughts swirl.
Darkness can hover.
The clouds roll in.

Cute gets thrown out the window.
No time for cute when the water is rising.
The serious side comes out.

Bubbly, fun Karen has a seat.
And serious, analytical Karen stands on up.
She is still gracious and kind.
But, in these moments?
There is no time for cute, I'm afraid.

Honestly, I think the serious side comes out way more than the cute.
My people know this.
They see me like this more often than not.

Thinking.
Contemplating.
Worrying.
Remembering.
Believing.
Looking for Truth.
Asking if any of this real.
Looking to see Jesus in all of it.

Maybe it's just all part of growing up?
The childlike cuteness doesn't get as much playing time.
Bench that cute little thing.
Bring on the heavy lifters.

There is a whole lot of seriousness in this life.
A whole lot of heartache and pain.
And fear is real.

Tragedy comes.
Life happens.
There is a time for all of it.

The oral surgeon struck a nerve while numbing me the other day.
I thought I was going to shoot right up through the roof.
Lots of deep breaths.

He told me it was all ok.
Then he asked me if I was ok.
I reluctantly said *yes?*

Then I asked him if he was ok.
I was serious.

He thought that was really cute.
His nurse did too.

So, maybe just maybe, there is room for both?

how would i explain my anxiety?

Well, for the most part, people would not know I have it.
Day to day, on the outside?
It's all good.
I'm all good.

Here's what I told Kevin this morning.
It's like a low rumbling on the inside.
A gasket that could blow at any moment.
Just the right prompting.
Just the right thought or feeling?
And here I go again.

I told him when I get really anxious about my health,
I just want to cut that part of my body off.
Sounds extreme, I know.
And I also know that it wouldn't help,
Because the next time it would be another part of my body that I'm fearful of.

Then I asked him if we can maybe just cut out the part of my brain that is so stinking OCD?

Nope.
Not today.

I know that the very same part of me that makes me feel anxious...
And darn near knocks the wind out of me sometimes...

Well, that's the part of me that makes me a good cheer/majorette coach.
I see things differently.
Little things that others wouldn't pick up on.
I obsess over free hands, feet being together, and arms being straight.

So, if you cut out the part of my brain that obsesses over every freckle?
You lose a part of me that can coach with the best of them.

If you take away the imagination that can conjure up the worst possible outcomes for my life and the life of those I love?
I would probably lose the dreams, visions, and possibilities of what God just might be up to.
Does this make sense?
I'm not saying I'm this amazing coach or dreamer.
I do think there is potential for that, though.

Potential...
At age fifty-two.
Yep.
Seeing beyond the crazy.
Looking through all of the obsessive and seeing the good.
Realizing there is room for me and my brain in this world.
A need for brains like mine.

Learning more and more every day, how to control the thoughts.
Learning to love how God made my brain.
Appreciate it.

Figuring out how to not beat myself up over the fear and frenzy.
Breathe into the low rumble.
Maybe even thank God for it.

Wow.
Just writing this feels freeing.
I could learn to be thankful for all of this?

Rest for my soul.
I say this so much.
I just want rest for my soul.
Maybe the resting will come with understanding how to be grateful for all of it?

I've identified with a life of anxiety for twenty-seven years now.
Always longing to be free.
Always hating this part of me.

Being ashamed of the fear.
How can I love Jesus and be so stinking afraid?

How about at age fifty-two... starting to see it all as a gift?
Leaning in and being grateful?
Who is with me?

a love story

I'm ready to change the narrative.
I've been thinking through this for a while now.
Not even sure how to type it out.
I will try though.

Thirty-two years ago, around this time,
I found out I was pregnant.

This became such a huge part of my story.
And for good reason.

My whole life got turned upside down.
Both mine and Kevin's.
The months that followed were hard.
We were not even twenty years old.
Scared would be an understatement.

Did we handle it perfectly?
Of course not.
Who would?
I'm not even sure what perfect might have looked like in this case.

As the years went on, we used our story to prove a point.
Told our testimony to so many.
Shared it in high schools and churches.
At banquets and in bible studies.
A beautiful story of redemption and grace.

But here's the deal...

When we would share it?

We always told it in a way that painted us in a pretty bad light.
It was important to let kids know not to try this at home.
Yes, God is amazing.
Yes, He made something pretty fantastic out of our screw ups.

However,
Do as we tell you to do, not as we did.

I understand why we said this.
I get that a lot of the times things don't work out.
And we went through a whole lot of pain during those years.

But, right now?
I just want to tell our story from a different angle.

There is actually a love story in all of this.
One that hasn't been told for fear of causing another to stumble.

I told Kevin all about it this morning.
Then I picked up my computer.

He smiled,
Gonna write about it?
I smiled right back,
Yep.

It was the summer of 89.
Kev came home from college.
He asked if I wanted to "hang out/hook up" for the summer.

~ Sidenote ~
*We had always been friends with benefits.
Started kissing behind the little red barn
in my backyard
when we were in the 8th grade.*

I really never saw myself "dating" Kevin Shock.
He was just a good friend,
and a darn good kisser.

So, we hung out together,
almost every night,
and somehow it got serious.

We started going on real dates.
Just the two of us.
Dinner and a movie.
Late night talks in his car
while we ate Big Macs or Taco Bell.

He sent me roses...
Just because.
Our little fling was becoming
more than a fling.

Here's where it gets crazy...

I asked him to go to Nationals with me.
Baton Twirling Nationals.
My parents said he could come along,
and then his parents said he could come along.
I know, right?

Guess where this contest took place.
Scranton, Pennsylvania.
I know, right?
We knew Scranton before Scranton was cool.

The day of the competition,
I remember sitting outside of the school,
right on the edge of a beautiful mountain.
The scenery was stunning.
And Kevin was so cute.

We talked about deep stuff that day.
I felt so close to him.

He was my biggest cheerleader when it came time to compete.
I still have a note that he wrote to me, telling me to "be intense."

Our team won the whole thing.
We were National Champions.
Total elation.
So many tears.
We had worked hard and it had paid off.

Kevin Shock was right there for it all.
He was precious.

That evening, in the hotel, our team had a victory celebration.
It might just have been one of the best days of my life.

And later that same night?
It happened.

Our little Alyssa was conceived.
In Scranton, Pennsylvania.

~ *Another Sidenote* ~
Kevin noticed on this trip that I had blue eyes.
He let me know that he had always wanted a blue-eyed baby.
Oops.
I thought he was gonna get just that.
Can I tell you?
Four children later?
Not one of them has blue eyes.
Jokes on him.
They all look identical to their father.
I wouldn't have it any other way.
And... we do have some real cute blue-eyed grandbabies.

I didn't find out for a while that I was actually pregnant.
I may have been late, but I was in denial.
By the time I did find out?
Kev and I had broken up.
We were both heading off to separate colleges,
ready to pursue separate dreams.

He was devastated when I showed him the positive test,
and we fought for pretty much the entire pregnancy.
We were both so young and so scared.

Kevin came to see Alyssa when she was born.
I remember looking over at him as he held her,
just the three of us in the hospital room.

Tears began to fall from his eyes.
She looked just like him.
He will tell you,
in that moment,
his life changed.
He knew he wanted to be a dad.

We still had so much to figure out.
Lots of talks about God and life came after that.
Trying to make it work.
We were just kids.

Our families were so gracious.
They came around us
and walked us right through those first few years.

We got together and then broke up.
Got together again,
and then broke up.

There was so much to work out.
And God did just that.

Worked it out.
Changed both of our hearts in so many cool ways.

We went from being a young couple of kids,
to a couple of kids with a kid,
to a married couple of kids with 3 more kids.

Things were not perfect.
Our story has had many ups and downs.

We are still a couple of kids.
With a pretty fantastic love story.

And I see now, more than ever before,
how God was in the whole thing.
The whole messy,
crazy,
beautiful thing.

c-section

My emergency c-section broke me.
Twenty-eight years ago.

Things seemed to be so under control.
Pretty perfect labor.
I had this.
I was rocking the whole Lamaze thing.
Kevin was proud of me.
I was proud of me.
I was a natural birth champ.

Until I wasn't.
After an hour and forty-five minutes of pushing?
I was done.
Our baby was in distress.
I needed a c-section.

They told me to stop pushing until
the anesthesiologist got there.
And I lost it.
No more control.
Worst pain of my life.

No idea how long it went on.
Seemed like forever.
I just know... I lost it.
I was so scared.

In so much pain.
Screaming and crying.
No more a champ.
Out of control.

Finally, the anesthesiologist came in.
I remember his big blue eyes.
Scolding me.
You have got to work with us, Karen.
I hated him.
No really, I think I hated him.
Then, I remember he said, *nighty night!*
Then... black.
Until I woke up later in my room.
Kevin was in tears.

They think Andrew (our newborn son) has a broken blood vessel on his brain, or an aneurysm, or something.
They are sending him to Toledo.

Toledo was an hour away.

Wait... what?
Please, someone wake me up from this nightmare.

Three days recovering in Defiance Hospital without my baby.
The pain was intense.
I had never had known that kind of pain.

So many tears.
Those days were driven by fear.
My hospital room seemed dark and lonely.

Everyone was going to see Drew in Toledo.
I wanted it that way.

But... I was alone.
In pain.

Our little Andrew ended up being fine, btw.
Turns out the anesthesia got into his system and caused some temporary apnea.

Fast forward to one year later.
Almost to the date.
I had my first panic attack.

Heart palpitations and chest pain.
I didn't know what it was at the time.
I just knew I was terrified.

Correlation?
Umm... probably.
Counselors think so.
I think so too.

The scariest part for me was the loss of control.
This experience broke me.
Sent me on a journey.

I think I just like to be in control, ya know?
And since that day?
Well, I've understood just how vulnerable we all are.
How fragile this life is.

No matter how hard I try.
No matter how much I plan.
Life takes twists and turns.
And it's scary.

My journey has been one of anxiety which leads to depression.
I can look back and see where it might have come from.
A PTSD of sorts.

But no matter where or when it started, it came.
And I have struggled.
And I have seen God in the struggle.

I have met amazing people because of it.
I have grown in it.

Wandered off the path, and came back.
Leaned into Jesus.
Relied on friends.
Grappled with life and death.
Questioned God.

And dreamt of a day when I would no longer be afraid.
Honestly?
Not even knowing exactly what I was afraid of.
I'm seeing clearer now.
The fear of losing control.
A control that was never a reality in the first place.

So, I'm learning to take one day at a time.
Be in the moment.
Trust God with today.
This day.
Finding rest in today.

how did i become brave?

What makes a person courageous?
It's all about the hard stuff.
Life happens.
And it pushes some of us over the edge.

For me?
It was anxiety and depression.
Back in the 1900's.
Before it was ever really talked about.

I kept telling my doctor I was having a heart attack.
I for real thought I was dying.
I was in my mid-twenties and in pretty good shape.
He ran all the tests.
So many tests.

He looked right at me in his office and said...

It's not your heart.
It's not your heart.
It's not your heart.

I shook my head in tears.
It had to be.

He then told me it was depression.
Nope.
Not depressed.
Except the dang tears running down my eyes as he said it.
Still though, I didn't "feel" depressed.
Anxious?
Sure.
Not sad though.

He began to explain how the two go hand in hand.
Anxiety and depression.
But it was so very physical.
The chest pains and heart palpitations.
The dizziness.
The feeling like I was going to faint.

C'mon Doc, figure it out.

If it wasn't my heart, it had to be cancer,
because I knew I was dying of something.
I just wanted to know what it was.
I'd never heard of anxiety/depression killing anyone.

But there I was.
It was all so embarrassing.
All the doctor appointments.
The medications.
Having to stay with my mom and dad so they could help with the kiddos while Kevin worked.
I couldn't get off the couch.
But how could it be depression?

Sidenote ~
I used to think I was failing my children with all this selfish sickness stuff.
Which made me even more anxious.
I know better now.
Our kids have made it clear how much they loved those days/nights at their grandma's.

This is good news for any young momma who walks this journey.
Your kids will be fine.
Hang in there.
Let others help.
They aren't feeling what you are feeling.
My kids were drinking grape pop and playing cards with Grandpa.

Ok, back to being brave...

I didn't choose this.
I would have gladly passed on the whole anxiety struggle.
But it has taught me something.

I'm so very human.
So very dependent on God.
Dependent on others.
Not even close to being perfect.
Couldn't even pretend to be when I couldn't get off Mom's couch.
People knew.
And I became ok with them knowing.

Because I realized most people cared.
They somehow understood.
Some even told me they had the same struggle.

Me... being vocal about it?
Was actually helping others know they weren't alone.
Or at the time, even just know that there was such a thing.

This road has been long.
And I know this is something
I will probably deal with for the rest of my life.
It's been twenty-seven years.
I can do another twenty-seven like this.

So much has been learned about it.
Medication and meditation help.

A good counselor is a must.
And being vocal about it doesn't hurt.

This anxiety journey has helped me see how honesty is the key.
And it has taught me to be honest about a bunch of other things as well.

Where I am in my faith.
How I feel about this life.
What I am learning about God.
All the questions I have.

You see, the more I put it out there, the more freedom I find.
I want to be loved for who I am.
Not who I am pretending to be.
Not some version of me I think you will like.

Just me.
The real me.
And the bonus is?
When I tell you who I really am?
And you still love me?
Wow.
There is just nothing better.

Let's learn to be real with each other.
This is where we learn how to be brave.

from one brave momma to another

I have a photo from 20 years ago,
holding my sweet baby Lance.
It's been one of those pictures I kind of hate to look at.
If we would have had digital cameras back in those days,
this picture would have been erased.
Can we all say re-do?
Chin up.
Different angle, please.

But here's the deal.

I've been learning how
to look at the beautiful
and the true parts
of my life.

It's so easy to look at all the wrong we do.
My mantra has pretty much been...

What is wrong with me?

Saying these words all day long...

What is wrong with me when I don't feel good?
What is wrong with me when I feel lazy?
What is wrong with me when I blow it with my kids?

And here's a big one...

What is wrong with me that I had to have c-sections?

So here I am.
Working through it.
Writing a book about my life with a new narrative.
The true and beautiful.

Recently, I found out that my great grandmother died in childbirth.
She and the baby didn't make it.
My grandma was two years old at the time.
She lost her mom when she was two.
I had no idea.

But there is something
I've heard many times since giving birth...

Well, at least you could have c-sections.
Back in the old days, women died giving birth.
You could have died.

Yeah, yeah, yeah.... whatever.

Until I opened up our family's genealogy book.
Reading it honestly took my breath away.

My great grandma gave her life.
Giving birth.

She was one brave woman.

And you know what?
Me too.
I am too.

I'm changing the narrative.
I bravely got through that first emergency c-section.
It wasn't pretty.
There was a fifteen-minute period when
I thought I was going to die.
And feared for Andrew's life.

But...
I lived.
And I chose to have more kids.
Knowing the risk and the pain.

And I can't help but think...

My grandma and great grandma were watching over me in all of it, cheering me on.

And you know what else?
Since then, several mommas have actually
wanted me in their hospital room with them
as they welcomed their babies into this world.

I have cheered them on.
Helped them breathe.

One brave mom,
cheering another brave momma on.

who am i to judge

The problem with my weight,
has never actually been my weight.

It's been how I've perceived my weight.
It's how I've looked at my body.
It's what I've seen when I glance in the mirror.

Immediate yuk.
All the flaws.
The thoughts just flood in.
The judgment is harsh.
And my mood tanks.

I've learned recently that there are lots of people who won't even look in the mirror.
I do look.
And I judge.

~Sigh~

But, can I tell you something?
It's getting a whole lot better.

You see, over the past couple of years I have put on some pounds.
Around twenty of them.

A few years ago, I did the whole Keto and fasting thing.
I lost weight.

Everyone told me how great I looked.
I kind of even told myself how great I looked.
It was easy to think the thinness would make me happy.
It sort of did.

But my anxiety and depression went off the charts.
I actually wasn't so healthy.

My BMI was great.
My cholesterol went down.
But every time I stood up?
I felt like I was going to pass out.

What is wrong with me?
Do I have a brain tumor?
Am I having a stroke?
Is it my heart?
Something is wrong.

I just knew I was dying,
but I never put two and two together.

Turns out my brain wasn't doing so hot.
It needed food.
Carbs to be exact.
Oh, and some fat.
I just wasn't consuming enough of anything.

I liked the way I looked.
And I didn't want to lose my confidence.

Gaining weight?
Not an option.
Eating enough food?
Not an option either.
Until it had to be.

My blood counts were off.
My doctor told me to stop the diet stuff.
Deep breath.

You mean, I have to choose?
Yep.
You can still eat healthy but you need to eat.
Feed your body.
She is starving.

So, I began to feed her.
I indulged at first.
My little body wasn't sure what was going on.
It was kinda fun.

And then it started to catch up.
The weight began to stick.
My pants started shrinking.

And I began to worry.
If I don't control this more?
Where am I gonna end up?

But you know what else was happening at the same time?
The fog was lifting.
My hair was growing.
My cycle normalized.
And I was just plain happier.
Oh, and the dizziness was gone.

All the things.
All the things that matter, that is.

Turns out my brain likes food.
My experiment with being skinny had failed.
And I am grateful.

You know, my mom and dad weren't skinny.
They enjoyed life.
They ate good food with good friends.

Mom cooked the best meals,
with a whole lot of butter.
She ate cookies for breakfast,
and Captain Crunch Cereal, with honey on top.
Candy was her best friend.
And she lived to be eighty-nine.

I'm ready to give up the fantasy of being some kind of model at age fifty-two.
No time for that I'm afraid.

I want to feel good.
Listen to my body.
Eat ice cream with my hubby.
And pizza (crust and all).

I realize I still need to stretch, walk, and lift some weights.
Add some veggies and fruit to my meals.

Most importantly though?
I will look in the mirror in the morning and give myself a high five.
Look myself in the eye and say "We've got this."
And move on.

I will stop judging myself so harshly.
And focus on others.

I will lean into life.
Trusting in Jesus all the while.
Resting in the body he gave me.

No more scales.
Whatever it takes.

Living, loving, and growing.
Even if it requires new clothes?

That last sentence made me smile.
Smiling is my favorite.

Stop typing, Karen.
It's time to eat some lunch.

just a kid

My favorite name.
Dad called me *Kid*.
So did Aunt Ruth.
My brother Bill still does sometimes.

Kev does a lot.
I like when he says it.

Why?
What feelings does it bring up?
Being called *Kid* and *Kiddo*?

I just think it makes me feel safe.
Protected.
Like someone older and wiser cares about me.
Knows me enough to call me *Kid*.

I'm the baby of our family.
And I admit... I like it.

But I will say I have spent a good amount of my adult life
trying to figure out what is going on with the kid inside of me.

Just who little Karen was, and still is.
What makes her afraid and what brings her life.

Understanding how it all fits into who I am today.
What I believe about the beautiful, terrifying, amazing world we live in.

Life is a journey.
I know I've written a whole lot about mine.
Just a kid.
Living in an adult body.
Longing to understand and be understood.
Discovering what it means to love and be loved.

And maybe?
Just maybe?
Encourage another kid along the way.

a good home

If someone says just the right word?
It can send me into a spiral.

It can happen to anyone.
Trigger words.

Recently, my niece just brought up the word *Findlay*.
A town about an hour away from where I grew up.
Mostly, Findlay just makes me think of the best pizza in the world.
Jac & Do's Pizza.
I can almost taste it as I type.

But, also?

I think of the time when...

I was nineteen years old.
Pregnant and not married.
Living with my parents and going to college.

In the Christian world this was a big sin.
Not the baby part.
The getting pregnant part.

A baby "out of wedlock."
I cannot stand that phrase.
I was having a baby,
And I wasn't married.

I had so much support from my parents.
I also had a whole lot of judgement,
from well-meaning people.
Everyone had an opinion.

People said things...

She made her bed, now she can lie in it.
What will she do now?
Is she going to give the baby up for adoption?
If she loves this baby, she will give it a real family.
This baby needs a mom and a dad.

I even had my sister's friend ask if I would give my baby to her.

Did I mention?
My parents were there for me,
every step of the way.
Dad and Mom were all in.
It was all the other voices.

I wanted to do the right thing.
I actually loved this baby more than my own life.
This little human growing inside of me.
I would sing to her at night in my bed.
I still have a journal of letters I wrote to her.
I adored this little one.

So, I went to counseling.
Went through all kinds of workbooks.
Read stories of other young girls who had given their babies up.
I learned how hard keeping a baby was.
How expensive it was going to be.
All the heartache I was in for no matter what decision I made.

Then I went to Findlay.
Me and my friend (who was also pregnant).
We both packed our bags to go live in a home for pregnant unwed mothers.

The plan was to stay there until after we had our babies.
Having the people who ran the place help us decide what to do.
Keep or give our babies up for adoption.

The house was nice.
The couple in charge were really sweet.
Lots of rules.
Lots of bible studies.
Lots of talking about life.

Guess how long we lasted?
Not even a week.

Here's why.
The other girls who lived there?
They were all keeping their babies.
And not one of them had the kind of support my friend and I did.

They were trying to figure out where to live and how to afford it all.
They were also getting dressed up in their mini-skirts and walking down to the local jail to meet guys.
I am not kidding.
You can't make this stuff up.

I called my parents and asked them to come get us.
My dad came to our rescue the following day.
I had decided to keep my baby.
I'm pretty sure God used this little trip to Findlay to show me I was going to be ok.
Help me realize how much love I was surrounded with.

At this point I settled into the fact that I was going to be a mom.
We bought a crib and put it in my bedroom.
Pastel rainbows and teddy bears all around.
My family had a baby shower for me.
Little onesies and neutral outfits.
Bibs and bottles.
All the things.

And I had a baby.
Without knowing what the future would hold.
Not having a clue that the father would walk back into the picture.
Not knowing how this would all play out.
Just a simple knowing of how much love I had for this little lady.

I held her in my arms.
My sweet Alyssa Ann.
I told her over and over how much I loved her.
I still tell her.

She is thirty-two years old now and has her own sweet family.
And when I hear the word *Findlay*?
For just a second?
I go down the road of what my life would be like if I had given her up for adoption.
And the tears fall.

Now, don't get me wrong.
There are so many beautiful stories of adoption.
I'm just saying,
It doesn't have to be everyone's story.

If it were up to my parents, I would have never even considered it.
They never pressured me once to think this way.

It was the pressure from other adults.
The ones who thought the only route would be to give this child a mother and a father.
Two parents who are secure in life and in their marriage.
A good home.

My home though?
It was a pretty darn good home.

A village raised our little Alyssa.
And I'm so glad we did.

PART II

journals for days

They go way back.
I was feeling anxious the other day and decided to look back through some of them.
Just to see if I normally feel this way at this time of year.

So many prayers.

Top Ten Lists...
My top ten prayers that would take a miracle to see God answer.
I've made so many of them.
Anxiously writing.
Begging God to do the impossible.

I can honestly say that most of those prayers were answered.
Not all, but most.

So many of them were me...
Crying out for mercy in raising my kiddos.
Sleepless nights.
Laundry issues.
Too much T.V.
Homeschooling.
All the things.

Please Lord, make me organized.
Make me a Proverbs thirty-one woman.
I want to be a better wife, mother, friend, daughter.

Make my anxiety go away.
Help me to trust you.

I don't want to live like this anymore.
I need a miracle.

Oh, and take away my selfish heart.
Why do I have to make everything about me?

Thank you for today, and for my life,
But please change everything about me.

This isn't quite how I wrote it.
I've always been much more polite and spiritual.

But this is just how it came across as I read today.
Me... begging God... for a different me.

And as I read?
I realized thirty years into journaling,
I am still wanting a different me.

It's easy to do.
Look at the ideal.
Hear sermons about the quiet woman of God.
Look at all those around me who don't struggle with anxiety.
And wish for a different me.

But... what if?
What if the me that is me, is really the me that God loves and enjoys?
The me that relates to others?
Understanding their pain?

What if?
I already have it all.
What if the thing I'm looking and crying out for is right here inside of me as I type?
What if I already have all I need in this moment?
With all my flaws, and selfishness, and anxious stinking thoughts?

Let's help each other.
Let's look each other in the eye.
And tell each other that we already have the abundance we are so desperately seeking.
Right here,
Right now,
Loved by God.
The God who gives us all we need.

dramatically reasonable

Over the top.
Panicky.

I know this about myself.
I've always had a flare for the dramatic.

You can see it in my seventh grade diaries.
Big words.
If a boy said "hi" to me?
Well, "I almost died."
Or… "had a hernia."
Didn't even know what a hernia was.
Still don't.

But I know I am still this way.
Pretty much, anyone who knows me, know this.

It made me a good cheerleader.
And it makes me a good cheerleading coach today.
Loud and proud.

Full of excitement.
Dreaming big dreams.
Ready for fun.

And then there is the dark side of it all.
The freaking out.
The panicking.
Making more of a situation than it really is.

Worst case scenarios are always in the back of my mind.
Maybe even the front of it.

I hear an ambulance?
It has to be somebody I know.

Someone is running late?
Probably in a ditch.

I get it.
Not everyone is this over the top.
And the world needs some of us "over the toppers."

But I really do want to work on this.

To be able to stop and breathe.
Maybe even be reasonable?
Understand the difference between good, fun drama and flat-out panic.

Still ready to jump on the bed with the grandkids.
Dance in the kitchen.
Sing into a spatula.
All those things.

And then...
When the real live drama comes?

I want to learn to be the calm.
The voice of reason.
A peace in the middle of the raging storm.

Maybe I could even be known as
Karen "not freaking out" Shock.

It will take a whole lot of work.
Some major deep breaths.
Probably even a dang miracle.

But... What if???

What if God could do this inside of me?

Reasonably fun.
Reasonably calm.
Reasonable.

Quick to listen, and then slow to speak.
Bringing a certain peace with me wherever I go.

Fun, with a flare for peace.

This is my prayer for today.

the shame of it all

After a tear-filled counseling appointment,
my therapist looked at me and said...

I think we've struck gold.

I've been in the midst of this anxiety journey
for almost twenty-eight years.
Lots of therapy.
Tons of prayer.
Bible studies.
Podcasts.
Prozac.

Never wanting to shy away from it all.
Always being willing to dig a little deeper.
Shovel some more dirt out of the way.
Willing to put in the hard work to get to the bottom of this struggle.

She reminded me of how I say...

I'm afraid but I don't know why.

I say that?
Yep.
Apparently, I say it quite often.

So, yesterday?
We went a little deeper.

Shoveled on past the fear.
Kept digging.

Wanna know the gold?
The thing behind the thing?
The thing under the thing?

It's... *Shame.*

I had told her several different stories of older people,
who had said some hurtful things to me in the past.
You see, when you are vulnerable,
and put yourself out there,
and reach out to people about your fears?

Well, sometimes even the most well-meaning people?
Shame you.

I told one older woman I was afraid to get cancer.
She looked me in the eye and said it was because my identity wasn't in Christ.
It was in my looks.
I was vain.

I told another older woman about my fears.
She looked me in the eye,
and flat out told me,
I was flipping God off.

Oh?

I'm vain.
And,
I'm flipping the god of the universe off???
The one I am coming to, on my knees, begging for healing?

Yep.
Giving him the old bird.

Ok.
There is one more.

I was telling a group of people about my hypochondria once, and the older gentleman sitting across from me said...

You know, God can heal you of your eye problem.

I freaked out.
Could he tell just by looking at me that I had some sort of eye cancer?

Nope.

Turns out, it wasn't that kind of "eye."
It was actually an "I" problem.

As in, I thought about myself too much.
After I told my counselor this story, I asked her if I am a narcissist.
She said I am not.
Then, we went and dug some more.
How about the two times I threw up in elementary school?

Once in art class and once all over my third-grade teacher's desk, dress, and grade book.
As I told both of these stories, I began to cry.
Ugly cry.
Little first and third grade Karen.
Ashamed.
Which led to being afraid.

Hmmm...
I spend a whole lot of time being ashamed.
I'm even ashamed at how many times I've said "I" in this book.

Ok.
Not really.
Not anymore.

If I can tell you all about my stuff?
Maybe it can help you see some of your stuff.

Which reminds me, she said my vulnerability can make people not like me.
She told me that if I want everyone to like me, I need to stop being so vulnerable.
I asked her why.
She said when I am vulnerable, I become like a mirror to others.
Other people can actually see themselves in me and sometimes they don't like it.

Wait, what?
It isn't really about me?
It's more about them?

I know now there is something to this shame stuff.
And that is one thing I haven't ever thought of.
Oh Lord, have mercy and help us see.

Shame puffs up the fear.
Shame is like the air that is blowing up the balloon of fear.
I'm so scared because I am ashamed.
I'm terrified because I don't want to be ashamed.

When really, there is no shame in any of it.
Let's remind each other of this.
Nothing at all to be ashamed of.

purity

Pure.
Holy.
Clean.
White as snow.
Fresh.
Beautiful.
Clear.
Unblemished.

A culture of purity.
A movement.

Where adults taught the young people the importance of it all.
How to "stay pure."
How to think pure thoughts.
Find a pure partner.
Keep a pure heart.
Stay this way for Jesus.

Sex?
Don't even think about it.
Not even a hint.

Kiss it all goodbye.
Kiss sex goodbye.
Kiss holding hands goodbye.

Better than all of that?
Just kiss dating goodbye.

Pure.

Not only on the outside.
Make sure you are pure on the inside as well.

Don't give your heart away.
Keep your heart to yourself.
Guard it.

Save it for your future spouse.
You know, the one you aren't thinking about.

Why?
Well, because...
Hearts get broken,
with the opposite sex,
before it's time to be married.

Once you are married?
Well then, have at it.
Give your heart away.
To the one you are married to.

If you do all of this?
The promise is bliss.

Wait.
Not from God.
The promise isn't from God.
It's from us.
The ones who are telling you to do this.

Not that we did this.
It was impossible.
And our hearts got broken.
And we want your hearts to be intact.

Whole.

Never mind that a friend could actually break your heart.
Or your pastor could break it.
Or someone in your own family.

Don't worry about those kinds of broken hearts.
Only the sexy kind of brokenness matters.

So, focus on this.
Put all your time and energy into this.

Think about it all the time.
Think about how you aren't supposed to think about it.

Wear a ring to remind you not to think about it.
Wear it all the time.
So, everyone knows you aren't thinking about it.

Sign a commitment card.
Pray about it all the time.

Oh Lord, help me not to think about it.

Don't think about it.
Don't think about it.
Don't think about it.

Dang it.
Why am I thinking about it?

I should spend more time trying not to think about it.
Less time thinking of others.
Less time dreaming of ways to help others.
Less time serving others.

I won't think about joy, peace, love, patience, kindness.
I can't.

I'm too busy thinking about not thinking about sex.
Or even any kind of relationship with someone I'm attracted to.

Nope.

Don't be attracted.
Don't look.
Keep your head down.
Blinders on.
No eye contact.
That's for sure.

And if you do have any feelings?
Keep them to yourself.

At least pretend you are "pure."

As long as it looks like you are?
Well then, that's about all we can ask of you.

Don't think about it.
Don't think about it.
Don't think about it.

Dang it.

an apology (from a true love waits leader)

I'm sorry.
I see now the damage that was done.
Standing in front of you sweet kids.
Telling you to do what I hadn't even done.

Giving you the little purity talk.
Having you sign the True Love Waits commitment card.
Handing you a TLW Bible.
Putting a purity ring on your finger.

We were pushing the purity culture agenda.
Making it seem like it was the cure all.

Those videos we had you watch?
They were driven by fear.
I can still hear Pam's voice in my head.
It was just fear mongering at its finest.

I looked her up the other day.
She is still the same.
Spreading the same message.
And just as angry as ever.

AN APOLOGY (FROM A TRUE LOVE WAITS LEADER)

Why did I like it?
How could I have not seen?
Again, I'm so sorry.

I dumped a heavy burden on your backs.
One that no one should ever have to carry.
It breaks my heart when I think about it.

Telling you all that it was your responsibility.
Making you believe your bodies were nothing but a sexual temptation.

Don't cause your brother to stumble.
Watch what you wear.
How you walk.
How you talk.
Those boys are weak.
You be strong.

The message was all kinds of messed up.

Don't kiss.
Don't date.
Don't even think about any of it.
Not even a hint of sexual immorality.

Ugh.

Just so you know, I'm having a hard time forgiving myself.
I've been in therapy for it.
Wanting to take back those evenings.
Get you all together in one spot to ask for forgiveness.

Hearing the stories of regret.
The guilt and shame you have carried for years.
Into your marriages.
Into your relationships.
Into your adulthood.

Some of you are forty years old now.
Having kids of your own.
Trying to figure out what to say to them.
Wanting to tread lightly so they will not be scarred.

What I have learned more than anything else over these years?
Perfect love drives out fear.
Fear doesn't drive out fear.
God's kindness leads us to God.
Not fear.

Jesus said his yoke was easy.
His burden was light.

We told you Jesus loves you.
And then gave you a yoke that never came from him.
A burden you were never meant to carry.

I'm so very sorry.
I am humbled beyond words.

I put stipulations on God's love for you.
Conditions on God's grace.

Instead of the ring being a comfort?
I know now it became a source of condemnation for so many.
A constant reminder of failed promises.
Ones you should have never been led to make.

I did this.
I take ownership for my part in it all.

I know better now.
I know more than ever that I don't have all the answers.
And when you know better?
You do better.

AN APOLOGY (FROM A TRUE LOVE WAITS LEADER)

God gave us our bodies.
Our sexuality.
Our desires.

I tried to take it all away.
Believing it would keep you safe.

God wants us to free.
Free to love and be loved.

I want my story to be one of declaring this love.
No more burdens.
No more being defined by our sexuality.

Defined by love.
That is all.
Defined by love.

we gave grace...and then took it away

I remember one brief moment in our evangelical days.
When we did some crazy, cool things in the name of Jesus.

A group of us had the privilege of coming alongside a homeless community.
We told them all about the grace and love of God.
It lasted a sweet minute.

Then?
We started telling our homeless friends what *"not"* to do.

All the loving... led to leading.
Straight into the same bondage we had been living in.

We gave grace... and then took it away.
Jesus loves you... now don't drink anymore.

Did we give them rest?
How could we?

If we wanted to prove their new found faith?
They had to get their act together.

If we wanted to bring them into church?
They needed to clean up a bit.

And round and round and round we went.
The vicious cycle of "don'ts."
I became dizzy.
Which made me anxious.
Which led to depression.

And then to doubt.
Not to doubt in Jesus.
But to doubt in the system.
The institution.
The church leaders who were making the rules.
Laying heavy burdens on all of our backs.
Teaching us to lay heavy burdens on each other.

So, I asked questions.

You know how they answered?

Don't ask questions.
Don't lead others astray.
Don't scare the children.
Don't make us look bad.
Oh, and don't make Jesus look bad.

They just couldn't handle it.
But I couldn't help it.

And I know now that Jesus could/can handle it.

You see,
It's his kindness.
It's his love.
His grace and mercy.
His peace that passes all understanding.

This is where my hope is.
This is where my rest is.

In a God who leads us by still waters.
Into greener pastures.
A more expansive life.

Loving, giving, serving.
Expecting nothing in return.

Do you know how nice it is to expect nothing in return?
Not trying to "sell" anything anymore.

There is no system for me to sell.
Instead, there is a love I can freely share.

An unconditional, never-ending love.
My thoughts are not ridden with guilt and shame anymore.

And the more I realize this?
The more I want to share it with the world.

i was told not to trust myself

This is what I was taught.
When we were deep into reformed theology.
Nothing good in me.
Therefore, nothing to trust.

My thoughts?
My intellect?
My instinct?
My heart?

Nope.
Trust none of it.
Don't lean on your own understanding.

But then, whose understanding do I lean on?
Where do I go for wisdom?
Answers to life's biggest questions?

Oh, right.
The scholars.
The ones who "know" the Bible.
The older men who have seminary degrees.

Look to the commentaries.
Make sure you have the right ones.

The ones we tell you to read.
The versions we learned from when we went to school.

Stay in our lane.
Listen to us.
And anyone else we say you can listen to.

Don't go outside of our circle.
Stay here.
Read this.
Not that.

Listen to this podcast.
Stay away from the other ones.

Talk to this person.
Not that one.
Go to this school.
Stay in our denomination.

Because, of course,
we are right.

Even though it goes against your gut instinct.
Stick with us.

But, wait a minute.
How do I know you are right?

Because you are my pastor?
My elder?
My leader?
My covering?
I need to trust you?

How does that work?
You get to be trusted…
But I cannot trust myself?

Because of your degree.
Because of your position.
Because of your intellect.

Hmmm...

What about your dang heart?
Why do you get to be trusted?

Because you decided you would go to college to be a pastor?
So... now you are "anointed."

Does this anointing make your heart trustworthy?
Does it give you some kind of wisdom I cannot get?

Is your version of the Bible or some commentary the "right" one?
Is God more willing to give you the truth than me?

How does this work?
I have all the questions.

I am so very tired.
Tired of being told I cannot trust myself.
Tired of being told I need to trust what someone else tells me.

How they see scripture.
How they interrupt it.
How they know which version is the "right" one.
With no accountability in what they are teaching.

I remember sitting with my husband, across from our pastor.
With tears running down my face.
I held out my bible and asked him what the heck I was supposed to do with it.

One of the leaders in our church was a "scholar."
Therefore, he knew the Greek and Hebrew.
And this leader had told me
I could not trust my interpretation

because I was just...
Well, just me.
A young mom,
without a degree in theology,
and apparently without a brain.

Ok, no-one said that to me.
But it did feel that way.

Come on in, and leave your common sense at the door.
Don't be bringing any of your "wisdom" in here.

We've got the corner market on that one.
We are anointed by God.
No need for you to think or anything.

You might wanna leave your emotions at the door as well.
No time for that, I'm afraid.
None of it is trustworthy.

Bring your babysitting skills,
cooking skills, and decorating skills.
We need that stuff.
But honestly, we don't need your thoughts.

So, where am I now?
How do I feel about it all?

Here's how...
It's all poppycock.

God made us all with brains.
With hearts and souls.
He gave each one of us instinct.
And more importantly, the Spirit.

I no longer live in fear that God is some big,
old professor in the sky,
just waiting for me to fail a test on theology.

I am no longer trying to find the right group
of smart guys to hang with
so I can get a good grade.

And I am so thankful.
Because, more and more?
Those old white guys I used to follow and trust in?
So many of them are failing.
Not the just theology test,
but they are failing the *living like Jesus* test.

Seeing people for who they are.
Loving.
Serving.
Listening.
All of these kinds of things.
The "Fruit of the Spirit" kind of things.

More and more, it seems they are the bullies in the school cafeteria.
And I no longer will fight to sit with them.
I will stay on the outer edges.
Find a different crowd.
Not the popular ones.
No time for that, I'm afraid.
I have begged to really know God for years.

And I'm realizing now...
The way to know God?
Is to humbly be still.

And believe the love that has been put in my heart,
is a love put there by God.

I can trust it.
I can trust the part of me that longs to see goodness.
The part that longs to lift others up.

See the good in them.
And tell them the truth about
who God made them to be.
Beloved.
Free.
With a heart to love and be loved.

Let us lived loved.
And let us trust our instincts to love one another.
Thank you, God...
for making us with a heart to know you.

i used my depravity as an excuse

Wait...
I forgot to put the word "total" in there.
Total Depravity.

As in?
Complete.

All.
All of me is depraved.

Nothing good in me.
Not even an ounce of goodness.

So, what did anyone expect?
The bar had been set really low.

The words *I'm a loser* came out of my mouth quite frequently.
A young momma,
dripping with four small children,
and a severe case of anxiety/depression.

Here's an example:

Kev asked me to clean at least one pair of his underwear.
For real, he wasn't asking for much, bless his heart.
I however, couldn't seem to get that one little task done.

Oops.

And when he asked me about it?
I didn't just say *I'm sorry*.
Instead, I told him what a loser I was.
An all-around loser.

Which, in my head, was more than true.
Looking back, it was one heck of a cop-out.
No apology.
Just a blanket *I'm a loser*.

He honestly wasn't being a jerk about it.
And I wasn't being a jerk back.
It wasn't a case of *Do your own dang laundry*.

This isn't about that.
This is about me, continually calling myself a loser.

Ok.

So, let me take this whole depravity talk one step further.

I would tell our children they deserved hell.
Yep.
It was all part of our theology.
We actually learned to say this.

If one of our sweet littles
would ask for something he/she couldn't have?
And then proceed to whine about it?

I pulled the old *You know what you deserve, right?* card.

They knew.
They knew the answer.
They deserved nothing.
But... Hell, of course.

I was a good momma.
I loved them something fierce.
They were my life.

And it was important for them
to know how dang depraved they were.

Ugh.

If Jesus chose them, then they would be ok.
No eternal torture for them.
Which is what they deserved.
So, we would pray and ask Jesus to choose us.
But we knew we had no control over any of it.
And if he didn't choose us?
It's fair, because we all deserved Hell.

And then I rocked them,
and sang about How great our God was.
Oh, and then the guilt of loving them too much
would come creeping up on me.

Do I love them more than I love God?
Oh no.
I think I do.
I've made them an idol.
Now he will have to rip them away from me.
Put himself back up on the throne.

I know all of this is so depressing.
But this theology is so depressing.

And I lived it.
I walked in it.
I taught it.
Until I couldn't anymore.

Until the day came when I opened my eyes.
Looked around.
And cried *BS*.

This cannot be who God is.
How in the world is this God?

Things began to unravel.

And although it was painful?
It was/is the best thing that has ever happened to me.

Waking up to a loving God,
and a loved Karen.

Realizing I can see Jesus
by looking in the face of my child.
It's not about loving them too much.
It's about seeing them as the gift they really are.
Good gifts.
It's starting with Genesis 1 instead of Genesis 3.
God made us and called us "good."
Let's start there.

It helps to know there is good in us.
I see it.
We are all made in the image of God.

Do we mess up?
Of course.

Do our kids mess up?
Yes.

But can we see the good in them?
Can we look for the good in others?

Do we need Jesus?
Yes.

It's his love for us that causes us to love others.
We love because he first loved us.

So, I am learning.
Every day.

To see God in a new way.
To see myself, my kids, and my grandkids in a new way.
To love and be loved.

The label is no longer loser.
The label is beloved.

let's not grovel

Have you seen the movie **Ever After**?
The Cinderella story with Drew Barrymore?
The scene where the prince puts the slipper on her foot?
It's not like the other Cinderellas.

You see, she is so dirty.
Her hands are dirty.
Her clothes are dirty.
She looks kinda smelly.

And yet?
The prince asks her to be his bride.
I cry every time.

Ok, stay with me.
What if?

What if after she becomes the princess,
she spends all her days telling
the prince how unworthy she is?

She grovels.
She gets on her knees and
continually tells him she doesn't deserve him.

At some point...

Wouldn't you think he would tell her to stop it?
Wouldn't he want her to live into her position?
Be grateful, but also enjoy being his bride?

See where I am going with this?

We all have been saved by the prince.
The Prince of Peace has come to seek us out.
He loves us.
We are his.
If he owns the cattle on a thousand hills?
I guess we do too.

Can we be grateful?
Yes.

Should we grovel?
I'm thinking... no.

Can we tell others about this Kingdom
and the love the King has for us?
Each and every single one us?

Yes.

I no longer like the words *Believer* or *Christian*.
If someone says... *so and so isn't a Believer?*
I say back...

They just don't know how much Jesus loves them yet.
If they knew?
They would believe.

If we could live into our true identity,
and really understand God's love for us?
We would be freed up to love,
and tell others they are loved as well.

Some days though?
I just want to grovel.
Tell myself and others what a dang loser I am.

When this happens...
Will you please speak the truth to me?
Tell me I am loved.

And when you feel the same,
which you will,
I'm gonna speak that truth right back to you.

You, my friend, are loved.
We are loved.

PART III

loved and accepted

~ Today, I Karen, commit to discover and experience all the ways I am loved and accepted. ~

I had to write this out every morning.
With my right hand three times.
With my left hand three times.

Seems silly, right?
Kind of not silly at all.

Here's why.
Several years ago, I was telling my counselor
about how I've always felt like a "misfit."
How I even want to write a book about it.

In tears, I told him how I think this is why
I have such a heart for the marginalized,
the bullied, and the people
who just feel like they are
too different to fit in.

I said I really want them to know
they are not alone.
I am for them.
God is for them.

He then got real with me.
Really real with me.

*How can you give to others
what you don't know for yourself?*

Oh.
Oh no.
Oh no, you are so right.

He told me it was time for me
to stop looking for all the ways
I am a misfit.

To stop looking for the ways people don't like me.
To stop telling myself I am one.
To stop saying it out loud.

He asked me to take a minute
every day to focus in on how
I am loved and accepted.

By God? I asked.

*Yes, by God,
But, also by others.*

He told me to start looking for it.
Almost like a detective.

Man, I'm so drawn to look for the negative.
To wonder what people think,
and assume they think the worst about me.

Does this make sense?

It really came to life for me
as I began to do this exercise.
No, like... really.

I started to see how much
family and friends seriously do love me.

They weren't doing anything different.

I was.

My focus changed.
My thoughts turned around.
I found myself smiling
a whole lot more,
leaning into the positive,
and realizing that I can also help others
feel loved and accepted.

I can point them to a God
who fully love and accepts them.

I can teach them how I'm learning
where to put my thoughts.
And how to change my mind.

May we see ourselves as God sees us.
May we live in the light of God's love and acceptance.

May we stop assuming we are misfits.

May we look for the good in others,
and be more aware of the good they see in us.

May we start believing we are loved,
and accepted right where we are.

being a lifelong learner

I still have so many questions.
There are still so many questions.

Do you know what I love about it?
I love how God puts people in my life to teach me.
Different people.
All the time.

We can truly learn something new every day.
From anyone and everyone.
It's especially fun when they are younger.
Humbling.
And fun.

Honestly, our grandkids teach me all the time.

Kessa is so smart.
She is a wealth of new knowledge if I'm just willing to listen.

Liv teaches me how to not take life so seriously.

Alice teaches me how to take it more seriously.

Axel J.?
Ummm… he teaches me that I can't run as fast as I used to.
Also humbling.

How about our own kids?
Young adults.
They know so much about life,
and they are not afraid to speak into mine.

Maybe it's about my fears.
Sometimes it's about today's culture.
Lots of times they school me on who God is.
Again, humbling.
I mean, really.

I should stinking know more than they do.
And sometimes I do.
But, a whole lot of times?
I learn from them.
I simply ask "What's up in your life?"
And they share.

And I've gotten really good at listening to them.
Not so much so I can tell them how to live.
Or show them how much I know.
Nope.

It's more because I have so much to learn.
I think they know that.
Kevin is good at it too.
Listening.
Learning.
Growing alongside of them.

We believe in them.
These next generations.
The ones on our coattails.
They are learners too.

I sometimes wonder if our kids are such good learners
because they see us still learning.
Does that make sense?

Ok.
How about the older people in my life?
I've always loved having mentors.
Someone older and wiser to speak into my stuff.
I still do.

When someone with more experience in the world
tells me it's all going to be ok?
It means everything.

What means even more?
When they believe in me.
Encourage me to be better.
Point me in the way of Jesus.
Show me how to live like him.

Oh, and guess what.
Jesus asked questions.
Jesus led by example.

When his disciples wanted to push the children out of the way?
He wasn't having it.
Let the little children come to me and do not hinder them.
For the Kingdom of Heaven belongs to such as these.

He saw value in them.
Absolutely.

So, going into this new school year?
I want to see the value in these kids.
I want to learn from them.
Let them know they are teaching me.

And maybe, just maybe,
they can learn a thing or two from me as well.

freedom to be different

Alyssa and I were part of an important discussion the other day.
It was a long time coming.
I had my listening ears on.
Believing she was about to speak some truth into my life.
She was gracious with her words.
She is pretty terrific about saying hard things in a loving way.

It all started when our extended family was sitting around the kitchen table talking about parenting.
Discussing how everyone could do better in this area.

We were chatting about the whole "Fun Heilshorn Family" aspect of life.
She brought up the time we were at Cedar Point.
She was nine.
I pretty much made her ride the Magnum.

Oops.

She hated it.
I honestly thought she would love it.
We all did.
You know, part of the "fun" our family had.
Once again,
she hated it.

And here's the deal...
I've said I was sorry many times since then.
I knew I pretty much scarred her that day.

But, on this day?
She was ready to explain why it made
such an impact on her little life.
You see, she was just trying to fit in.
Be part of the built in "fun" that our family was all about.

She told me how it wasn't about rollercoasters.
Rollercoasters were not the point.

Space.
Space was the point.
Letting her have the space to be who she was.
The person she was created to be.

She explained just how hard it can be to "fit in" with our family.
It even went so far as her letting me know how
a whole lot of times it felt more like a moral issue
than just a preference.

Alyssa is a perfectionist.
Pleasing her parents was,
and still is very important to her.
And somehow?

I made her feel different.
But not in a good kind of way.
She felt like she didn't fit in.
She just wasn't fun enough.

The whole table began discussing the way our family
can make a person feel like an outsider.
Our way is best.
The way we eat, sleep (or don't sleep), drink, vote, worship God...
And so on and so on.

We are just pretty much,
well... right.
We are right.

Oh, and then my nephew Kevin pointed out...
There is also not much room for any discomfort.
This comes directly from our matriarch.
Mom never wanted to see anyone sad.

No time for sadness or pain.
Fix it at all cost.
Everyone should be happy.
If you aren't?
We will do what it takes to correct it.

Please, please, please...
Just be happy.
Our happiness depends on yours.
Oh, and also...
Follow us.
Believe just like us.

Don't color out of the lines.
Don't go getting creative with your thoughts.
Don't listen to anyone else.

Stay inside the lines.
Then you will be happy and we will be happy.
Be good. Behave. Be one of us.

Our little tribe.
I mean, if you are different, we won't shun you.
But we will make faces of disapproval.
We will discuss it with you.
As well as behind your back.
Because we have to figure out how to get you back in line.

To our family,
let me just say this...

I'm sorry.
I am sorry for thinking my way was/is the right way.
For all the times I've tried to talk you into being something you are not.
For all the times I've discouraged you from doing any critical thinking of your own.
For the times I haven't listened.
For the pride of thinking I know best.
If I want to be free to think for myself?
It is only fair for me to give you that same freedom.

I understand that being a parent means we guide and direct.
But dang it.
I am learning to humble myself before God
and, also before you.
Freedom is what we were made for.
How can we best live free
and help others to find that same freedom?

For today, let's listen to each other.
Give each other some space.
Space and freedom.

when this happens...then

We live our lives like this.
My days go like this.
My nights go like this.
Because my thoughts go like this.

I can rest when...
I will be happy when...
Everything will be better when...

So, when actually is... when?
Does "when" ever come?

I will have joy when the weekend comes.
I will finally be happy when I get married.

Nope.

How about when I finally get pregnant?

Nope.

When the baby is born.
When the baby sleeps through the night.
When the baby is out of diapers.
In school.

Out of school.
On their own.

How about...

When I get the job.

When vacation comes.
When I retire.
New house.
New car.
Famous.
This amount of money.

This number of followers.

And it goes on and on and on.

So, here's what I'm learning...

We have now.
This is what we have.
I have today.

And the happiness I am looking for?
The joy I'm hoping for?
The peace?

It isn't about what is out there.
It's not about the "when."

Jesus is inside of me now.
The Holy Spirit resides in me today.

The possibility of love, patience, peace, kindness, etc.
Is on the inside of me.
Not outside of me.

Not something I have to continue to strive for.
Looking for love in all the wrong places.

Love is here.
Love is now.

I remember hearing someone say once...
If you want fun, you've gotta be the fun.
Oh.
I can actually be the fun?

Can I actually be the love?
The peace?
The joy?

Well, if the God of the Universe resides in me?
And God is love?

Then maybe, just maybe, I don't have to look too far.
Maybe, just maybe, for today?

I have everything I need for life and Godliness.
I may just need to sit in it.
Rest in it.
Believe in it.
Walk in it.
Abide in this truth.

Jesus.
Right here inside of me.
And in you too.

Deep breath.
Now, let's go have a day.

defining moments: encouragement for the weary mom

Could my depression have been caused
by being a "stay at home" mom?

The long days of same.
The never feeling quite like I measured up.
Oh, and the *I'll do it tomorrow,*
Because, you know...
Tomorrow is the same as today.

And when the depression and anxiety set in?
I started believing that I couldn't be out in the real world.
I wouldn't make it out there.

Depressed people don't do well out there.
Anxiety in public would be awful.

It would be better to just stay in.
Try to pray away the anxiety and depression.

And as the years went by,
I watched it become a part of my identity.
That was me.
Twenty-five years of staying home with the kids.

Some getting out and coaching,
but it was only in short spurts.
I will admit though, it felt good to get out a bit.

For the most part,
I was at home,
feeling all the guilt of a messy house,
a mountain of laundry,
and meals to cook.
Oh, and then there was homeschooling.
A constant bombardment of thoughts about not being good enough.
Never doing enough.
Kicking my own butt in my head.

And then?
My kids grew up and I went to work.
I dressed myself up and went to work.
And it felt so good.

And people were nice.
And the two o'clock hour came and went without a hint of me feeling the afternoon blues.
I came home and realized something.
Maybe all these years were not about me being weak.
Maybe the depression and anxiety were a product of my environment.

It would be so nice to know this to be true.
Kev and I discussed it.
We did laundry together and discussed it.
We had to get the laundry done,

because I wasn't going to be home during the day to do it,
or to stare at it.

It felt good to just do it.
And I told him how I felt a sense of newness.
An excitement building about our future.

But also, a sense that if I could go back?
I wouldn't change a thing.

No wait...
There is one thing I wish would have been different.

I so wish I would have had an older momma...
Telling me that the depression is just kind of a side effect of staying home.
That it's hard and it can bring with it a sadness.
The afternoon blues.

But then, she could have also told me that it is all worth it.
And to hold on.
These days would pass.
And I would be able to function out in the world.

The season I was in wouldn't last forever.
And my babies would grow up and someday understand the sacrifice I made.

That is just it.
It always felt like I was just lazy.
I didn't realize I was sacrificing anything.

Staying home in my sweats,
wiping noses,
and staring at the piles of laundry?
Felt...
Lazy.

People would say...
Oh, I could never homeschool my kids.

And I would think...
I stinking can't either!

But I did.
They are all grown up now.
Graduated.
They all hold their own in this world.

I didn't feed them the best food.
And after I messed up their laundry enough?
Each of them started doing their own.
I'm not even kidding.
Turns out, that if you turn their whites pink a couple of times?
It actually motivates them to do their own.

Oh, and I rocked them.
All the time.
I rocked them while I sang songs loudly,
trying to make them (and me) feel better.
My kiddos watched me struggle through those years with anxiety/depression.
I think they even rocked me sometimes.

We walked those decades together.
And now they are all out and about.
Living and dreaming.
Schooling and working.

And our Alyssa is taking the same path as her momma.
She is so much better at it than I ever was.
She loves those sweet babies with every ounce of her being.
She has a schedule and they do school every darn day.

And like all the rest of us?
She has her moments.

So, to you Alyssa,
from an older momma,
I am saying...

Hold on!

Pray,
and rock,
and sing.

And just know...
The sadness you may feel during those long days?
It does not mean you are less,
or lazy,
or unfit for the outside world.

Those moments do not define you,
and they are so very worth it!

Ok... I've gotta run.
I have to go to bed.
I get to go to work in the morning.

the struggle is real

Our pastor's wife said something to me back in the day.
I was telling her about my anxiety/depression.
She said...

*It's fine if you struggle,
but your kids need to see you having victory over it.*

Oh great.
Well then, I'm ruining my kids.
Thanks for the encouragement.

And now comes the pretending.
I'll just pretend that I'm having "victory."
I'll just say that I'm healed.
Smile and move on.

Because I really need my people to know I love Jesus.
I really don't want to screw everyone up
by telling them I have pain.

If my children don't see me "winning?"
They won't be winners.

Of course, *It's Biblical to not fear.*
Just be Biblical, Karen.

Certainly, don't go on Facebook and tell
all your friends from the past and present
what you are dealing with.

It may cause them all to stumble.
Happy face.
Never let them see you sweat.

I'm good.
Aren't you good?
God is good.
So, I must be good.

Except?

When I'm not.
When I don't have it figured out.
When my past failures are staring me straight in the eyes.
When I bully myself with my thoughts.

I love my kids.
I love my family.
I love the people who are reading these words.
But hear me, I no longer believe it is love
to pretend that I am someone who I am not.

I'm not the *fake it til you make it* kind of person.
So here I am today.
Showing up.
Believing there are others
who need to hear
it's ok to not be ok.
Jesus loves us right where we are.

And we can tell our kids this.
Mom isn't ok,
but... Jesus.

And then?
When they are not ok?
~ Which will happen. ~
They will know they can be honest with us.

Right?
That's what we want, right?

Let's all be honest with ourselves,
our family,
and God today.

Honesty for the win.

we need each other

I watched Harry Miller in an interview today.
He was a football player last year for The Ohio State.
He was...
Until he just couldn't be any longer.

His depression and anxiety took over while he was playing.
And he knew it was time to quit.
For his own sanity.

He now speaks out about mental health.
Open and honest about his struggle.
The struggle is real.

I looked over at Kevin when the interview ended.
He had a tear running down his cheek.
Just from watching Harry's mom talk about it.
The pain she was in while watching her son suffer.

Kev related to Harry's mom.
I related to Harry.

Kevin then looked me in the eye
and told me he never wants to lose me.
He said it is just so hard to understand
how anyone could get so bad.

How anyone could ever even think
about taking their own life.

Here's what I told him...

When you are in your darkest moment,
and can't see a light at the end of the tunnel,
the guilt and shame sweep in.

It becomes so easy to think the world would be better off
if you weren't in it.

Your pain becomes too much.
Too much for you.
And you believe it's too much for everyone else.

You start to think...

*Life would be more fun for everyone
if I wasn't around to bring them down.*

It's a scary place to be.
And I'm so glad he got the help he needed.

There was one time when I felt this way.
When the cloud was so thick
I couldn't see a way out.

It honestly had to do with my medication.
The doctor had upped my dose.
It wasn't working.

Thankfully, I knew my thoughts were dangerous.
I called my niece.
She came over right away
and sat on my bed with me
while she made a couple of calls.

She called my doctor.
And then she called her therapist.
I had my first ever counseling appointment the next day.

It only happened that one time.
We still talk about it to this day.
I thank her for being there.
And then she thanks me.
For what?
For reaching out.
For being honest.
For staying here.

I wrote about it on Facebook
a week after it happened.
Some people felt sorry for me.
Others felt seen.

I understand.
And I'm thankful for both.
The ones who get it.
And the ones who don't.

We all need each other.
And we all need a chance to be heard.

no strings attached?

Kev and I were deeply committed to a church.
Four small children and busy lives.
We were on a strict budget trying our best to pay down debt.
People in our church knew this.
There were lots of us younger couples who were all in the same situation.

An older lady insisted on dropping groceries off to us.
I tried to say no.
She responded with...

Don't you stop my blessing.

Got it.
Understood.

We were so grateful for all the food.

And then it happened.

An elder of the church pulled Kev and me over to the side the next Wednesday night before youth group.

Here is what he said...

Someone saw you two at Applebee's the other night and we know that you received groceries last week.

Ummm...
Were we getting in trouble for spending money on eating out?

We told him we used a gift card we had gotten for Christmas.
Which was true.

But you guys, even if it wasn't????
How?
How was that ok?

We never asked for their gift of groceries.
We never asked for anyone's help.

I tell you what... it was awful.

The saddest part is?
We didn't even know at the time
just how controlling the whole thing was.

This was twenty years ago.
So why am I telling this story now?

Because I see well-meaning churches/people
still doing this type of thing today.
And it isn't right.
This isn't grace.

If someone gives any kind of gift?
No strings should be attached.

Let's not let people attach strings.
Let's not be people who attach strings.

I would like to think our little family learned from this.
I would like to think we know what it means to give freely.

My sweet momma knew how to give.
She would give the sweater right off her back
if someone told her it was pretty.

You want it?
I'll give it to you.
And she would honestly expect nothing in return.
She gave joyously.
I want to learn more and more how to give joyously.

May we all learn more and more what it means
to love
and give of ourselves
and our money...
Freely.

don't be confused, karen

God is not the author of confusion.
If in fact, if you are confused?
It's from the devil himself.

So, I shake my head.
Partly in disbelief.
Mostly trying to shake out the confusion.

Let me get this straight.
For real.

Don't love your life.
If you love it, you will lose it.

As a matter of fact, hate it.
Give it up.
If you give up your life for God,
you will find it.
Ok, then... I guess I hate my life.

Oh, but you should be grateful,
in everything.
In everything, give thanks.

But if I am grateful?
Wouldn't that mean I actually love something?

Maybe I should just be thankful for all the suffering stuff.
Because if I'm suffering?
I'm doing something right.
I'm losing my life.
Which means I'm actually finding it.

Yes.
I should suffer more.
And be thankful for it when I do.

Help me, though.

I love my kids.
I love them so much.

I love my husband.
I love him so much.

Dang it.
Probably too much.
What if I love them all too much?

You know?
I would rock my kiddos when they were little.
Holding them tight.
Singing and snuggling.
Looking at their precious faces
with tears rolling down my eyes.

I loved them so much it hurt.
Each one of them.
Part of the hurt came directly from what I was being taught.

Don't make them an idol, Karen.
Love them.
But, whatever you do, don't love them more than you love God.

Ok God, I love you more.
I promise.

DON'T BE CONFUSED, KAREN

I love you more.
I'm not sure how to do it.
But, please take my word for it.

Thank you, Jesus.
Thank you for my husband.
I know I don't deserve any of this.

I am so blessed.
But, wait.
Not too blessed.
Not blessed so much that I love it.

I'm learning to put it all on the altar.
Surrender it all to you.
Love you more.

Love the creator way more than the created.
Don't get too close to the created, Karen.
God is a jealous God.

Love them.
Yes, love them.
But, not more than you love any others.
Don't love them more than you love your enemies.
And love God the most.

Ok, I love you the most, God.
I promise.
At least I think I do.

Please don't be mad at me for not understanding.
I'm trying.
I'm trying to surrender my life to you.
Put it all on the altar.
Give you my whole heart.
Give you all of my dreams.

I'm just scared.
And I'm confused.
You scare me, God.
Your people scare me too.
I scare me, for that matter.
I just want to love you better.
I want you to know I'm trying.
But you confuse me.
Can I say that?

Ok.
Deep breath.
Back up.
What do I know to be true?
Ok.
I know this...
God is love.
Yes.
I'm coming back to this.

So, here's where I am landing today ~

As I wake up and walk out into this world?
You, God.

You made us and you love us.
And most importantly?
You live in us.
If I am loving one of your created?
I am actually loving you.
If I love one of my children so much it hurts?
I am loving you.

You love me.
You love them.
And you are not a monster.
You are not on a dang ego trip.

It's your love that is beyond comprehension.
Wider, deeper, and higher than I can even imagine.
The love I feel for my children?
Doesn't even come close to the love you have for me.
Or for them.

So, me loving them?
Is actually loving you.
Me being grateful for them?
Is actually me being grateful for you.

You are not trying to trick me.
You are in fact, asking me to rest.
Rest in your love.
Rest in knowing you love to watch me love.

More than that?
When I do show love to people?
It's you loving them.

So, I can rock my grand babies.
I can hold them tight.
I can think my hubby is way cute.
And love him with everything I am.
And know in all of it?
You are somehow smiling.
You aren't mad.
I'm loving you when I love them.
And for that?
I'm grateful.

PART IV

be still and know

Not...
Ask a friend and know.
Read a book and know.
Consult with your pastor and know.
Talk to your family and know.
Scour the internet and know.
Watch the news and know.
Listen to a podcast and know.
Go to church and know.

Nope, nope, and nope.

Be still.
Quiet.

It's crazy how I've been forgetting to do this lately.
I'm a person who wants certainty.
I want to know.
To know
that I know
that I know.

So, I ask questions.
Consult others.
Search high and low for answers.
I search the Bible for the answers.

And what does the Bible say?
Be still and know.

How many times am I reaching out for something
that is right here inside of me?

Grasping, flailing, tossing, and turning.
Turning my music up louder to drown out the noise.

When what I need is to quiet down that noise.
Sit still.
Get in my closet and just stop.
Breathe and let go.
Listen to what's deep inside of me.

The Bible also says Jesus resides in us.
Him in us.
This is where my hope lies.
Why do I search outside of myself to find the answers?
Why am I so stinking concerned about what everyone else thinks?

Be still, Karen.
Be still and know.

perspective

Alayna and I went to get manicures together this morning.
I, of course, complained about my how chubby my hands are.
Like I do.
She told me they looked beautiful.
I probably rolled my eyes.
Then she sent me this text:

> *~ Mom, you have beautiful hands. Hands that have*
> *held mine, that have braided my hair,*
> *changed diapers, held babies,*
> *can make delicious monkey bread,*
> *written beautiful words,*
> *hugged so many people,*
> *wiped many tears, twirled like a champ,*
> *shown how to do many perfect cheer fists,*
> *and a lot more.*
> *Beautiful hands.*
> *With an awesome manicure.*
> *love you! ~*

You know?
It's all about perspective.
Thank you, Alayna.
Your words bring healing to my soul.

values

Everyone has them.
Each person, our own set.
Changing throughout our lives.
Depending on the season we are in.

So, my counselor asked me to name mine.
Not just off the top of my head.
She wants me to really think about it.
Write about it.
Talk about it.

Come up with a list.
Five - twelve values.
Less than five?
Not enough.
More than twenty or so?
Too many.
Condense my thoughts.

Make a list.
Draw upon my past, present, and future.
The very values that make me who I am today.

If I can figure this out?
It will help me stay grounded.
Almost like a lighthouse on a stormy night.
When the waves get rough and the night is dark.

When confusion is surrounding me like a thick fog.
I can look at this list.
Remember what is most important in my life.
Who I am and what I am living for.

I love a good assignment.
A time to reflect.
A chance to learn and grow.

So, with paper and pen in hand,
I begin to write.
At the top of the page it reads "Values."
And then I start brainstorming.

What makes me tick?
What gets me up in the morning?
Where am I going in this life?
And who am I taking with me?

Hmm…

Here's a quick sample:
Jesus
Words
Peace
Fun
Adventure
Family
Children
Nature
Encouragement
Mental Health
Freedom
Non-violent resistance
Truth
Eye contact
A good hug
Gratitude

Beauty
Aesthetics
Vulnerability
Honesty
Tolerance
Joy
Laughing
Creating
Dreaming
And so on, and so on...

My list is long.
I will condense it into some sort of themes:

Learning
Relationships
Spirituality
Beauty
Fun
Mental Health

I will keep the list in a place where I can access it easily.
You see, if these values are at the forefront of my mind?

When I get stuck.
When I'm making mountains out of molehills.
When dark clouds hover.
And I don't know the next step to take.

I can go back to the basics.
Pick a value.
And take one little step toward
cultivating this in my life.

Am I making sense at all?
Maybe this is actually one of my values?
Making sense.
Having people understand me.

I will put this under learning or relationships.
Both are very important to me.

Kevin is figuring out his own values alongside of me.
They look a little different than mine.

Organization is one of his.
So is music.

And as we figure this all out together?
We can learn how to love each other better.
Give space for our differences.
And team up on the ones we have in common.

There is beauty in all of this.
And organization.
No wonder Kevin and I are loving this assignment.

is this real?

Might be my favorite saying.

Sometimes I say it like this...
Is any of this real?
Is any of this really real?
Can this be real?
Is this real life?
What is this life?

I really do say these things.
Several times a day.
A mantra of some sorts.

Often, I add this to it...
Am I really married?
Did I really marry Kevin Shock?
Do we really have four children?
And four grandchildren?
How did this all happen?
Am I really fifty-two?
Are my parents really gone?

Ok.
Deep Breath.
I'll stop.
You get the picture.

But I do spend a whole lot of time asking these questions.
Maybe I should have been a philosophy major?

Not for one minute would I want my brain to be any different.
Not for one second would I want to stop the wonder of it all.

I honestly don't want to settle in.
Take any of this for granted.
Walk through this life with all the answers.

I'm seeing more and more how it's all connected.
How we are all connected.
Everything is spiritual.
Everything belongs.

Christ is in all and through all.
We are all in this together.

Quantum physics and mechanics are so interesting to me.
Science, pointing us to the beauty of connection.
Science, pointing us to the wonder.
Science, helping us see there must something
that is outside of what we can see with our own eyes.

This life.
My life.
Your life.
Our life.

Moving from moment to moment.
But what is the constant in it all?
In my fifty-two years?
Who has been there for all of it?

Well yes, God has.
But, also?
Me.

My memories, my observations, my situations,
my hurt, my pain, my view, my hopes and dreams.

This thing inside of my body that asks all the questions.
This consciousness.
Has been here.
Looking out of my eyeballs.

Seeing the world from one perspective.
Being taught to see the world from that one perspective.

But here's the thing...
I'm beginning to look around.

Not just simply asking the questions as a mantra.
Not just asking the questions to get a giggle out of one our kids.

But, realizing there actually is a rhyme or reason to everything.
There is wonder in all of it.

We are all connected.
God is really moving in and through each one of us.

Just know... you and me?
We are connected in this moment.
Somehow, connected.
And, I believe more and more,
that we can pray for each other.
We can lift one another up.
And it matters.
It works.

Is this real life?
Am I really typing?
Are you really reading it?
Can we actually make a difference in this world?

Yes.
To all of it.

Breathe deep.
Look up and out.
And may we all get caught up in the wonder of what today might bring.

i'm an orphan

No really.
I'm fifty-two years old and my parents have both died.

Maybe this sounds dramatic?
And I don't think this way very often.

But man, when I do?
It hits hard.
The reality of it.

Even when my parents were getting on in years,
I still felt covered somehow.
Protected.

It's funny...
I had actually become their protector.
But just knowing they were here?
Loving me?
Well, I didn't know it at the time.
I just miss it, that's all.

I loved snuggling up to both of them.
Did this until their last breaths.

I grew up with "older" parents.
It always made me afraid they would die.
My friends' parents were so much younger.
Mine were grandparents already.

I was an accident.
Or shall I say "Pleasant surprise?"
They had already pretty much raised a few kids.
So, I got it easy.
They were tired.
Busy.
And sometimes even forgot me.

I hear stories about them leaving me.
You know, **Home Alone** style.
It's all good.

And toward the end of her life,
when I would drop Mom off at different places,
She would say... *Don't forget me.*

Ummm...
*I'm not the one who
has had the "forgetting" problem, Mom.*
I never did forget her.

I really wish I could jump in our car
and just drive to wherever they are right now.
Pick them up.

Just a small visit.
Let them know how much I love and miss them.

Tell them about all the grandkids and great grandkids.
Maybe I would even dance with them.
Sing a little song.

Let them know that I will not ever forget them.

This is the week when they both were in our home on hospice.
Nine years apart.
But, September.

I have yet to listen to one of
Mom's old Alan Jackson albums.
I will.

She loved the song *Precious Memories*.
I get it now.
I will listen to that one.
I'm sure there will be tears.
And a gratefulness down deep in my heart.

I might be an orphan here on this earth.
But I know, that I know, that I know…
Somehow, I just know…
They are still with me.

I mean, have you seen my Punkie candy jar?
Have you heard me tell Orvie bedtime stories?
They left an imprint.
And precious memories in each of our hearts.

the faith of my parents

There were some years in there when I questioned it.
Questioned their faith.

I was wrong.
And I know better now.

But let me tell you how it all went down.

The questioning of their faith started
when I went deeper into Evangelicalism.
Bible studies and podcasts.
The importance of spreading the gospel to all nations.

Even losing your life if need be.
Jesus was worth it.

It was bad to collect sea shells when you retire.
No time for that I'm afraid.
John Piper told us so.
We definitely didn't want to get to Heaven
and present our shell collections to God.
He would not be happy.
There were people to be saved.

Quiet times were a must.
Praying with your children before bed.

Community Groups every week.
Singing with your hands raised.
Men's groups.
Women's groups.
Homeschooling your children.
Leading ministries.
Conferences.
Memorizing Scripture.
Confessing sins to one another.
Breaking bread together.
Coffee dates.

Oh yeah, and weekly dates with your spouse.
Women submitting.
Men leading.
All the things.

Side note ~
Did I mention the anxiety and depression that came along with it?

You see, we were in deep.

Oh wait, one more...

Blood is thicker than water, but the Spirit is thicker than them both.
So, pick church gatherings over your family every time.

See how deep?
And that depth was what led me to judge others.

Where was their fruit?
Where were the Bible verses on their walls?
Why didn't my dad pray with me when I was little?
Why didn't my parents tell me about the unreached people groups?
Did they even love Jesus?

I feel sick typing this.
Again, I know better now.

It took a whole lot of humbling for me to understand.
My Mom and Dad are with Jesus right now.

Not because they did the above list.
Simply because they were loved by God.

They knew it.
They understood it.

Not perfectly.
But, the fruit???
Holy smokes.
Love, joy, peace, patience, kindness, goodness.

All of those things.

It ends up that their simple life of loving and giving was way more a picture of Jesus than a thousand hands raised in a room.

Does this make sense?

They just lived it.

Mom would come into the living room from the kitchen to find us siblings arguing over "deep theological things." She would look around the room and say to us...

I'm so glad I don't have a clue what you guys are talking about. All I know is... Jesus loves me this I know, for the Bible tells me so.

She then would shake her head and walk back into the kitchen.

Oh Mom, you were so wise.
And your love for people was Jesus in the flesh.

You carried a song in your heart
and the Spirit of the living God inside of you.

And Dad, you showed me the unconditional love of Jesus.

When it's hard to think that God could possibly enjoy me?
I remember the tears that fell from your face as you watched
any one of us children or grandchildren perform for you.

Thank you, Dad and Mom.

Forgive me for ever doubting who you were.
For my arrogance.
For my ignorance.

Oh wow... and I know you do forgive me.
You wouldn't even think twice about it.

Once again, proving you actually can
collect sea shells and be Jesus at the same time.

rapture ptsd

Rapture anxiety.
There it is.
I have had it.
I think in some sort of odd way?
I still have it.

Not scared it is going to happen anymore.
Just scared of it bringing up the feelings.
All that went along with the ridiculous rapture talk.

In the fourth grade was when I first heard about it.
Watched a movie.
A Thief in the Night/A Distant Thunder.
Let me say it again...
Fourth grade.

Went along with my parents to a high school youth event.
New Year's Eve.
Sat in the back and watched in horror.

What is this?
People disappearing in the middle of the night.
Planes crashing.
Cars wrecking.
People reeling.

And then?
The people who were left behind?

Running.
No food.
Fires and death.

And then???
They had to choose.
Get the mark of the beast or get their heads chopped off.

That's how it ended.
The star of the movie up on the platform ready to die.
The sound of the guillotine.

Lord, help us all.
Ok.
Deep breath.

I just found the darn movie on YouTube.
Watched some of it to make sure I was remembering right.
Oh... I was.

My nine-year old self didn't miss a beat.
The horses, the barn fire, the men with guns.

~ Side Note ~
I didn't remember how incredibly horrible the acting was.
How cheesy the entire film actually was.
Cheesy and Horrifying.

I absolutely do remember the aftermath
of what this movie did to my brain.

I slept in between my parents every night for months.
Holding their hands.
Praying they wouldn't be taken from me.
Praying I wouldn't have to get my head chopped off.

It scared the hell out of me.
And made me want to tell all of my fourth-grade friends.

I needed to scare the *Hell* out of them as well.
I was so sure it was going to happen any day.
I just knew it would happen before I graduated high school.

All the signs were there.
All the adults in my life were talking about it.
I had better be ready.
We all had better be ready.
No being "left behind" for me.

Then I had children.
The "Left Behind" generation.
They didn't read the books.
They just had a mom who lived in fear.

Even if I didn't speak it,
they saw it in my life.
The anxiety of a God who
was more about terrorizing children
than loving them to himself.

Yep... I lived in fear.

What if they get left behind?
What if they have to go through the seven years of tribulation?
What if we are going through it now?
What if our social security numbers are the mark?

What if?
What if?
What if?

In the last few years my *What if?* has been changing.
I'm seeing everything differently.
Believing Jesus doesn't bring us to himself through scare tactics.
It's his love that draws us to him.
It's his kindness that leads us to repentance.

Learning theology.
Studying who God really is…
Has led me to believe that these movies were all a crock of…
Scare tactics to win people to Christ.
But which Christ?
The music and the verses that were
displayed in this movie were haunting,
the premise was ridiculous,
and the outcome was a bunch of terrified children.
I am not alone.
Others are beginning to speak out on this.

The PTSD from this movie is prevalent.
Adults.
Remembering all of the voices.
All of the scary nights.
All of the prayers lifted to a God who was going to
snatch up a parent and leave us behind.
Holy smokes.
Can we all start a big support group?

Those movies had more of a negative impact on my life
than Jason, Freddie and Michael put together.

I understand we do not know what the future holds.
But I do know one thing.
The God who holds the future?
Isn't out to scare little children into Heaven.
It just doesn't work like that.
God's love is better than life.

conspiracy theories

Why are Evangelical Christians so prone to them?

Why was I so ready to believe them?
Ready to take a stand for something/someone
having no idea what the truth really was?

While I was filling up our coffee pot this morning, it just dawned on me.

I read a meme last night which said Donald Trump is all about us trusting in God,
and Joe Biden is only about us trusting in the government.
Donald Trump is a "hero" because he "talks about God."
Joe Biden is the anti-christ because, well, he is a Democrat.

There it is.
Somehow Christians have become really good at
believing whatever comes out of someone else's mouth.

If they talk about God in just the right way…
We will love and support them.

It starts with our confession of faith, yes?
Did they say they wanted to invite Jesus into their hearts?
Did they come forward?
Raise their hand?

Make an outward expression of an inward decision?
Something like that.

It's all about the right words.
Say the right prayer.
Repeat after me.
Say this prayer and your name will be written in the book of life.

One little prayer gets you all the way into Heaven.
And I bought it.
Hook, line, and sinker.

For most of my life I believed it was about a prayer.

I actually had young people repeat after me.
And then I told them they were good to go.
They now had a passport to an eternity with Jesus.
It was all about the words.

And how about this one?
If someone says *I'm a Christian?*

We will buy whatever that person is selling.
We will do business with this person.
We will automatically believe this person is safe.
Get our car fixed by them.
Buy a cake from them.
Listen to their music.
And on and on and on and on.

Those of us who have said the prayer?
We need to stick together.

And follow our leaders.
You know, the ones who say all the right words?
We blindly follow... right into the pit of Hell.

I'm not talking about a "literal Hell."
Nope.

More like, Hell on Earth.
A place where anxiety and depression reign.
Where we learn to hate.
Become bitter.

And most importantly?
Fear everything and everyone outside of our circle.
The circle of people who have said a prayer.

Maybe, just maybe,
I'm oversimplifying it?
Maybe we would say it's about a prayer and about fruit.

But... What fruit are we talking about?
Love, patience, peace, kindness, gentleness, etc?

Or is it about the fruit of telling others to say the dang prayer?
The fruit of following the ones who tell us to say the prayer?
The fruit of listening to the music of the ones who have said the prayer?
Going to the right school with other people who have said the prayer?

How did we get here?
How did it come down to words?

When I read the Bible and Jesus tells us to
Love God and Love others.

He doesn't say to
Say a prayer.

He says to
Love.

This is how people will know we are Christians.
By our love.

I remember having a priest counsel
Kevin and me before we got married.
He told us that God is love.

And because we loved each other?
We could know that we know God.

I pushed back.
I pushed back hard.

Twenty-three-year-old Karen,
talking back to a priest.

It's not about loving each other.
It's about praying a prayer.

I truly believed I knew more than Father Ed.
I was mistaken.
And I kept being "mistaken" for years to follow.

Until... it happened.
Our pastor told us he had asked a person to explain "the gospel" to him.
And because this person was able to
describe a court room scene where Jesus took the penalty?
This person was in fact "a Christian."

Everything began to unravel for me.
God is up in Heaven,
writing our names down...
And if we say the right words?
If we get our theology correct?

It started feeling like
up was down
and down was up.

I would shake my head.
I would stare out my bedroom window
and wonder if there was even a God at all.

My world was falling apart.
Nothing made sense anymore.

And I'm so very glad the whole thing unraveled.

I started using the common sense which God had given me.
I stopped believing that words were the ticket.
I read my Bible for the first time without the framing I had been taught.
I saw Jesus.
I read about love.

His words got ahold of my heart.

Love one another.
Care for the poor.
Tell others of my love for them.
The Kingdom of Heaven is now.
Rejoice in this.
It's really good news.

Turns out, salvation isn't some words
we say to get a ticket into the pearly gates.

Salvation is here.
It's now.
He lives in us.

The greatest compliment one can give me?
I see Jesus in you.
Just a simple, *I see Jesus in you.*

PART V

the need for certainty

This is what messed with my head.
Still does sometimes,
although not near as often as it used to.

Growing up,
I believed I needed to be certain.
Sure of my faith.

Believe without doubt.
Unshakeable.
Unmoved.

The wise man builds his house upon the rock.
Not being blown by every little wind.
Maybe weak in my flesh,
but never weak in my beliefs.

That was all well and good.
Until it wasn't.

When I stayed on the fringes,
things were good.

Then I dug deep.
Started studying the Bible.

Learning theology and doctrine.
Reading book upon book.

Being taught about our total depravity.
How there is nothing good in me.
Nothing good in anyone, for that matter.

Oh, and that God chooses.
Some to go to Heaven.
Some to go to Hell.

For all eternity.

Let me say it again for the people in the back.
For.All.Eternity.

Yep.
God may or may not have chosen me.
Worse, yet?
God may or may not have chosen my children.
Huh?
And there is nothing I (or anyone else) can do about it.

Not all babies would go to heaven.
Some are headed to an eternal conscious torment.

And as I type, I wonder how in the world?
How does anyone ever believe this?
Can we not just stop and think?

I can honestly say I tried to believe it.
I tried to turn my brain off.
Blindly believing whatever
the man up front was teaching me.

Don't think, Karen.
Throw common sense out the window.
God's ways are not your ways.

But it wasn't working for me.
I would say to everyone around me,
Just think about it.
I would beg them to
think about it.

God is love.
That's what the Bible says.
How could that ever coincide with an eternity of hell?

They would tell me to
not forget about God being "just."

What is justice?
Didn't God make the rules?
Couldn't he have made different rules then?

Or not created anyone at all?
I cannot imagine having a baby
if I knew for sure that baby was
going to be burned for billions of years.
In the hottest fire.

Never ending torture.
Nope.
Just don't have the baby.

And there is no way I love more than God does.
There came a breaking point for me in all of this.

After years of questioning and worrying,
I had an elder tell me
I couldn't know if a little boy
who had died the day before
was with Jesus.

I was grieving the tragic loss
of this sweet little friend.

Trying to comfort myself,
and anyone else around.

Simply saying out loud how
grateful I was that the little guy
was in the presence of Jesus now.

Nope.

We can't know that.
We can only hope.
Hope that because his parents were "believers," he was chosen.
They were chosen, so hopefully he was too.

Ok, but even if he was chosen?
Other sweet littles ones are not chosen?
What?
How?
How could this be real?
Why would I want to believe in any of this?

I remember wanting to scream
with every part of my being.
I will never forget the pit in my stomach.

The constructs of my faith began to fail.

There was a realization that
my house was built on sinking sand.
Man-made doctrines.
Not on the love of Jesus.
Not on his teachings.

The blinders slowly began to fall off.
My eyes began to see more clearly.

For the first time,
there was freedom to think for myself.

To trust the God-given reasonableness
of my own thoughts.

Deconstruction was happening in my heart.
Before deconstruction was cool.
And I'm not saying it is "cool."
I'm saying it is necessary.

People have been tearing down
broken systems and constructs
since Jesus walked this earth.

He was the first deconstructionist.
Coming here to teach us
about love and freedom,
grace and inclusion.

Sending his Spirit to reside in us.
Counsel us.
Comfort us.
Free us.
And give us the wisdom
to know what is true and right.

Today, I am grateful.
For my own deconstruction.
For others who are on this path.

We aren't who people think we are.

We are not just "trying to get away with sinning."
Nothing in me wants to get away with anything.

I just want to know God.
Really know Jesus.
I want to surrender myself to the Holy Spirit.
Radiate joy.

Be filled with hope,
not with certainty.

Reconstructing for the rest of my days.
Building on the solid rock of Jesus and his love.
Being real about my questions and doubts.
And loving others along the way.
Oh, and believing God loves them too.

was my anxiety a demon?

This is what they told me.
No, for real.
The demon of fear was inside of me.
And this demon could be prayed out.
Exorcised.

In some strange way I believed it.
Maybe it was because I wanted the anxiety gone.
I didn't want to go the long route.
Just cast the damn thing out of me.
It would be easier than years of therapy.

So, there I was.
On my knees.
People laying hands on me.
Asking it to leave me.
It didn't leave.

This happened to me on more than one occasion.

I was also told the anxiety/fear was a sin.
My panic attacks were sin.
Can you see how this could send me spiraling?
Fear built upon fear,
which built upon more fear.

I was taught at one point
to pray through every bad movie
I had ever seen,
or bad song that I had ever listened to.

Again, there I was, asking God to forgive me
for knowing who Michael, Jason and Freddy were.

And being afraid that,
because I had seen those movies,
I had opened some kind of portal
which satan could come through.

Why wasn't God just healing me of all of this anxiety?
Maybe it was the Ouija Board
we played with when we were in high school?

How about all the trick or treating I did as a child?

Maybe the fact that I let my own kids trick or treat?

You have to know though,
they always dressed up in nice costumes...
football players and ballerinas.
No witches or goblins.
That was forbidden.

But I did let them go out
into the darkness of the night
on Halloween.
Maybe that was the portal?

So, they prayed over me.
Strangers.
People who really thought
if they just prayed hard enough,
if they recited enough verses,

the right verses,
I would be free.

The demon would flee.

And the more we all focused on it?
The bigger the monster became.
The more I tried to figure it out?
The more scared and insecure I was.

Fear trying to drive out fear.
Anxiety about being anxious.
And round and round I went.

Feeling like a bit of a freak.
And a big failure.

Fear was driving my life.
Fear stacked upon fear.

I memorized all the verses about anxiety,
and I recited them all of the time.

I begged the god I was scared of
to deliver me from being scared.

It never worked.
Because it doesn't work.

Fear doesn't drive out fear.
Perfect love drives out fear.

Fear doesn't lead us to repentance.
God's kindness does.

When I stopped worrying
about being possessed by a demon?
That's when I stopped feeling

like I was actually possessed by a demon.
Does that make sense?

Mom would always tell me to accentuate the positive.
I would roll my eyes.
And go on my way... accentuating all of the negative.
Shining a huge spotlight on my fears.

Telling everyone about what a sinner I was.
Believing I was literally
flipping God off when I was afraid.

I know better now.
I'm trying to focus on Jesus.
Up and out.

Ruminating on his love for us.
Leaning into his kindness and mercy.

He knows me.
He loves me.
He created me like this.
I was born this way.

A deep thinker, with a pretty terrific imagination.
And when it is used in a good way,
it can help make the world a better place.

But, spending all my days and nights
imagining there is something very wrong with me?
Declaring it must be some kind of demon?
Believing there is no good in me?

All of this?
Leads to anxiety and depression.
And round and round we go.

It's time.
Time to get off

the merry go round
of guilt and shame.

Time to stop
leaning on my own understanding.

God's love is way deeper
and wider
and higher
than we can comprehend.

There is nowhere any of us can
ever go to escape God.
The mercy and kindness
and unending love
just leads us
and follows us
everywhere we go.

This God is in all and through all.
Why do I fear?
Why am I downcast?
My hope is in the Lord.
God has me.
God has you.
We are safe.
We are loved.
We are held.

stay in the ranks

Do not seek help outside of this church.
Anything you need?
You can find right here.

You see, I was all set to see a counselor for my anxiety.
One that my doctor had recommended.
My appointment was the next day.

*Sidenote ~ It had been set up for a while
because this particular therapist was hard to get into.
He was a sweet, older gentleman who actually
had his office in another church building.*

I remember getting a call from
our pastor while I was grocery shopping.
Walking aisle by aisle
listening to him while he tried to reason with me.

He was telling me the importance
of staying within our church body.
I didn't need to go outside
to get help with my anxiety/depression.
There were enough good people
to get me through it within our group.

I was shaken by this.
My appointment had been scheduled for a while
and I was so looking forward to it.

It seemed right that I would go
to someone who was on the outside.
Especially since a whole lot of my anxiety
was coming from the inside.

Looking back, I'm so thankful
for my husband's wisdom on this one.

When I called Kevin to tell him what the pastor said,
he immediately shut it down.

You are going to this appointment.
You need help and not from inside.
We do not need permission for you to see this counselor.

Deep breath.
More anxiety.

Now I'm doing exactly what
I've been so stinking anxious about doing in the first place.
Going against the "authority" of our leader.

Ugh.
Do you see how messed up this was?
I shudder to think of how this all
would have gone had I listened to our pastor.

You know why?
Turns out, our pastor was right.
The thing he feared most?
Happened.

My counselor listened to our story.
Sat across from me as I wept.
Heard me saying there was no choice in the matter.

I told him over and over how
we couldn't leave this church.

We couldn't be seen as
Church Hoppers.

God would want me to submit.
I needed to learn to stifle my bigness.
Shut my mouth.
Sit down.
Definitely not raise my hands when I sing.

I had to stop rocking the boat.
So, after a few months of counseling?
We just got out of that boat.

Me and Kev.
Kev and me.

Left our friends and family
and went someplace else.
Hopped on over to another church.

Sidenote ~ not the church where my counselor was.
He had no agenda except my mental health.

I'm not gonna lie.
It was scary.
And so hard.

We were told by an elder that it
was like we were divorcing them.
Maybe so?
If you want to call it a marriage?
It was a very unhealthy one to say the least.

This was absolutely one
of the best decisions we ever made.
To this day,
I am so grateful to have a husband

who could see the situation
for what it really was.

All of this took place more than a decade ago.
Seems like a lifetime.
And yet, just yesterday.

I can still remember the insecurity I felt.
The hopelessness.
The raw emotions as I sat on that couch
across from a counselor
who knew exactly what I needed.

Being stuck and hopeless is no way to live.
And sometimes we might just need
people on the outside to speak into our situation.

I remember saying I felt like a caged bird.
The thing is?
The cage was never locked.
The door was always open.

It just took someone from the outside
telling me to fly on through it.
Oh, and can I say this?
It's so nice out here.

belonging

I've spent my life longing to belong.
To fit in.
The journey of a misfit.

What box do you want me to fit into?
Just tell me.
I will jump on in.

Oh, that one?
Ok.
It looks too small.
Are you sure?

Here I go.

Wait.
Maybe you should just put me in the box.
Because, God knows I'm trying to jump in.
I just can't seem to fit.

My legs are tired from a lifetime of boxes.
In and out.
In and out.

You really want me to fit into your box, though.
And I want to.
Because I like you.

Just help me.
Help me... help you
fit me into your box.

You keep stuffing me in.
I'll keep praying.
Trying to be smaller.

Maybe if I'm quieter?
Nope.
It's not working.

Your box is too small.
My big thoughts,
big dreams,
big hopes,
Just don't seem to fit.

Oh, but your box is the one God is in?
If I don't fit, then I don't know God?

Ok.

Just keep pushing me.
Beating me down.
Hammering me with "the truth."
If you make me small enough,
I'm sure I will fit in.

Shoot.
Hold up.
I forgot.

I'm actually claustrophobic.
You've got me all shoved in here.
But I promise you, I can no longer breathe.

There is no room here.
It's dark.
I can't see.

Maybe, stop telling me I'm fine.
Stop stuffing all my stuff back down.

I feel like a toy.
The old Jack-in-The-Box.
Keep winding me up.
Singing that same old tune.

Eventually?
I'm gonna pop on out.

And I will see.

Oh yes, I can see.
There is a whole world out here.
It's light.
And bright.
And there is plenty of room.
Air to breathe.

I can spread my arms out wide.
Look up at the sky.
Actually, unbox myself.

Because, it turns out?
God is outside of the box.
With all the other misfits.
Right here in our midst.

It's a big beautiful space.
With all different kinds of people.
So colorful.
So filled with love.

You told me that little box
was the only place where love resides.
Funny, I just felt trapped inside.

It's so good to breathe again.
To be me again.
Absolutely free again.

No more boxes.
No more silly games.
No more lies.

Out of the box.

toxic

I've been worrying for the past several years
about the toxins in our environment.
In our food.
In our products.
In our soil.
In our everything.

Except...
In our faith.

Toxic beliefs,
leading to nothing but fear.
Well, maybe not just fear.

How about being manipulated?
Or maybe controlled?
Shamed.
Abused.
I could go on.

Being taught.
And then teaching others.

Try to be pure.
But you are wretched.
But try anyway.

Submit to your authority.
But they are wretched.
But submit anyway.

Lead your wretched kids.
Tell them to be pure.
Not even a hint of immortality.
But you know they are wretched.

Make your home perfect.
Give your husband everything he needs to be perfect.
Husbands, make sure your wife is behaving.
Even though we all know she is a little wretch.

Watch your thoughts.
Take them all captive.
Every last wretched one of them.

No one is perfect.
No not one.
But strive for it anyway.

No wait…
Cease striving.
Strive to cease striving.

Discipline your kids.
Spank them for not striving.

Don't spoil them.
The little wretches need to be taught to stay in line.
To be perfect.
Except, they are little wretches.

Make sure we are all ready.
Ready for Jesus to return.
Don't be caught in sin when he gets back.
But know you are a sinner.

Ask for forgiveness.
And tell God you know how wretched you are.
Once forgiven?
Strive to be better.
To do better.

Don't be anxious.
What is there to be anxious about?
Except that he might return
when you are doing a bad thing,
and there will be nowhere to hide.

You are hidden in Christ.
Except when you die
and are judged
in front of God and everyone.

You are loved.
Unless you aren't chosen,
then, of course, you are not loved.

So, strive to let God know
you want to be one of the chosen.
Prove to him you are
worthy of being chosen.

Except no-one is worthy.
No not one.

And I look around.
And sometimes it seems like the people
who aren't in church understand
God's love way more
than the people who are.

These unchurched people?
Seem to actually rest easier.
Love without conditions.

Laugh more.
Judge less.

They seem to have way more freedom.
How is it that Christ set us free to be free,
but we are so quick to bind one another right back up?

We lay heavy burdens on others,
and on ourselves,
believing that fear will motivate,
and controlling others is the only way.

How about Jesus is the way?
His burden is actually light.
His yoke is easy.
We can actually find rest and freedom in him.
Not in all the rules and the striving.
In him alone.

Do I know what that all looks like?
Nope.
But I know it isn't what I'm seeing.
Not in the church.
And not in myself.

How do we do better?
By resting.
Actually resting.
Believing it is finished
and accomplished.
Christ is in all and through all.

Look around.
Look outside of the church.
Jesus is everywhere.

Look in the eyes of your neighbor.
Look in the eyes of your children.

Look in the eyes of your enemy.
You will see Jesus.

Let's get off the treadmill
of trying to be perfect.
Let's also get off the treadmill
of trying to convince everyone else they are wretched.
Oh, and the treadmill
of telling ourselves how wretched we are.

I'm tired.
This treadmill gets us nowhere.
Except maybe a life filled with anxiety.
The very thing Jesus came to save us from.

Oh Lord, help us stop the insanity of striving.
Help us live loved.
Help us tell/show others they are loved.

i can't unsee all i've seen

There's no turning back.

There was a time when I didn't know.
I just believed.
Just took what was said as Truth.

No digging.
No searching.
No questioning.

The music played.
I stood up.
I sang.
I raised my hands to the sky.
I mean, I raised my hands out to God.

The God in my mind.
The one on a throne up there somewhere.
Looking like Gandalf.

Just trying to reach him.
Begging him to fill me.

Show me.
Enlighten me.

Heal me.
Break me.

You know?
All the words.

I was desperate for him.
And I told him so all the time.

Sometimes it was with hands raised.
Other times it was on my knees.
On my face even.
On my face, on my dirty bathroom floor.
Crying out.
Change me, God.
Make me new.
Draw me close.

With every new song?
New words to cry out to him.

Maybe these words will get him to hear me.
Act on it.
Drive out those demons.
The ones named Fear and Anxiety.

Maybe, just maybe,
other people will use the right words.
Yes.
Lay your hands on me and pray for me.

Ask God to take away all the pain.
Heal my anxious heart.
I'm so scared.
Take it all way.

What will it take for you to take it all away, God?
I've memorized all the scriptures.

Quoted it to you more times than I know.
Thinking if I used your own words on you?
C'mon.
Why can't you hear me?
I'm begging.
I've been begging for 20 years.

Then the rug slowly began to get pulled out.
I began a different type of questioning.
Maybe this isn't God at all?
Maybe he isn't hanging out
on a throne up in the sky.
Maybe he isn't a man.

Maybe he isn't near as scary
as I've made him out to be?
Maybe he isn't as scary
as I was taught that he is?
Maybe he is Love.
And holds everything together.
And is in all and through all.

Maybe he is right here.
No, like... actually inside of me.
God in me.
Christ in me.
The Hope of Glory.
Living inside me.

And there is no need to grasp anymore.
Maybe there never has been.

He holds everything together.
Not with big giant hands.
More like glue.
Energy.
Connecting all of us.

I don't need to be afraid of some

cosmic being
who just comes to judge.

So, wait.

Could have my anxiety actually
been brought on by my belief
in who God was?

No, really...
Were my fears driven by my fear of God?

A god who causes people to get sick
and puts people in hell.

And the people who taught it to me?
Honestly?
They were just teaching what they had learned.

And scaring the hell right out of me.
Or were they scaring the hell right into me?
Now I'm shaking my head as I type.

Here's what I do know.

God is Love.
God holds everything together.
God is in all and through all.

There is a peace that comes
from deep within when I focus on this.

It doesn't come from outside of me.
No need to go outside of myself to get filled.
No need to beg.
Only to rest.
Only to realize.

This God?
Our Jesus?
He is right here.

In me.
In you.
Holding us all together.

Instead of praying for him to get busy hearing us?
How about we be still and know?
We all take a deep breath,
and remind each other of who we are.

Who God is.
Where God resides.
Right here.
Abiding in this love.

I raised my hands the other day.
Way up.

But not to beg.
This time, it was simply to say...

Be who you say you are God.
Right here.

Inside of me.

May I be the answer to someone's prayer today.
May I see you in them.
And may my mouth be filled
with the hope of your love.

willing to listen

I remember the first time
I decided to really listen.
Eight years ago.

It started with some podcasts.
Then I read a couple of books.
And one day, I got brave.

I reached out to my cousin.
Asked if we could chat sometime.

We hadn't talked since we were kids.
We were living in two different worlds.

I was a "sold out for Jesus" Christian.
He was a confident, strong, gay man.

It took some courage for me to reach out.
What would I even say to him?

Does he know I don't have a clue about him and his life?
Does he know I have erred on the side of homophobia?

You know, "love the sinner, hate the sin" type stuff.
I was never blatant about it.
It kind of wasn't my problem.

I was starting to learn some of the history
and my eyes were beginning to open.

A conversation with a gay person
seemed like what I was supposed to do.

So, I called Chad.
I honestly don't know what I was expecting.
He was so very gracious to me.
Patient with my silly questions.

But one thing he said still haunts me to this day.
What he said went something like this:

You Christians think you are so scared of us. What you don't know is, we are the ones who are terrified of you.

Hold up.
Why would you be scared of us?
We love Jesus.
We would never hurt anyone.

Oh snap.
Wait.
Would we?
Have we?

And the blinders began to fall off.
The hardness of my heart began to melt.

I decided that very day to be learner.
It was time to open my heart,
my mind,
my eyes,
my ears.

Tell me about your life.
Your pain.
Your worst fears and biggest dreams.

And God began to make a way for me to see.
A path to walk down.
One step at a time.

For the past several years I have been growing.
Learning.
Listening.

Some precious people have walked
straight into my life and heart.

My fellow cheer coach is like a daughter to me.
We have been through all the ups and downs
and all the drama that cheer can manufacture.
We have walked a whole lot of life together.

I love her.

She is not at all defined by who she loves.
We can talk for hours about all kinds of life.

She is just like me in so many ways.
As cheer coaches, we just kind of complete each other.

Last year, she got married to a young lady from my hometown.
Kevin and I went to our first lesbian wedding
in the mountains of Kentucky.
I pretty much just wept through the ceremony.
It was beautiful.
The whole day was.

And I'm so thankful
we have been invited to be a part of their lives.

Oh, and then there is our new friend Hammy.
This guy loves Jesus so much.
He can talk circles around us
when it comes to the Bible.

We started meeting once a week
just to get to know each other.
He challenges us in our walk.
He honestly points us to Jesus.
He is hilarious and smart.
And we are getting our worlds rocked by him and his faith.

I told him I want to be one of those ladies
who gives out "free mom hugs" at the Pride Parade next year.

He said he knows so many queer people
who he could bring to our house for me to hug.

He sounded like they just might need one.
And I am realizing now more than ever?
It would be way more for me
than it would be for them.
This momma needs some hugs.
Kev and me are in for the journey.
Wherever it may lead.

i lost my voice

I knew it was coming.
I went beyond the point of no return.
The slippery slope, as they say.

Too many questions.
Out loud.
If I only would have kept my mouth shut.
I tried.
Honestly tried.

The fear was real.
Fear of what people would think.
And fear of what I was actually thinking.

I was just done pretending.
But, my questions
were bigger than our church could handle.

Shhhh.
Don't say it.
Don't ask it.
Keep the dang thoughts to yourself.

Oh snap.

I'm saying it.
I'm asking it.
Out loud.

Let the chips fall where they may.
And they fell.

Speaking of chips…
I have never had a poker face.
Even if I would have kept quiet.
People would have known.

I was questioning my faith.
Which made me question my own sanity.

What is wrong with me?
Why can't I just believe?
More importantly, why can't I shut up about it?

Maybe if I just whisper my questions,
to the people I trust,
everything will be fine.

I'm fine.
I just can't believe that the God
we are worshipping would send people to Hell.

No really.
Why isn't anyone else questioning this?
A billion years.
And then another.

And he chooses who believes and who doesn't?
C'mon.

Shhhh…
Don't let anyone know you are thinking this way.

Ok.
One more though.
Just one…

If God uses us to tell others about Jesus,
and we aren't perfect...

And he let people translate the Bible
into something that isn't perfect...

Then why do we have to believe
it had to be perfect to begin with?

Stop it, Karen.
Just stop thinking.

Wait... one more.

Why would God make us love our enemies?
He doesn't have to love them...

But we do?

And doesn't the word **world** mean **world**?
And doesn't **all** mean **all**?

This was my brain.
My heart as well.

Reading all the books.
Searching all the commentaries.

Hoping to find a way to shut myself up.
Stay in the fold.
Keep my popularity.

After all, I spoke at women's retreats.
We were leaders of youth groups and college kids.

I had a nice little reputation for being wise.

Oops.

I just couldn't fake it anymore.

Funny thing is?
I knew God wasn't mad at me.
I knew God had ahold of my heart.
The God who created me gave me this brain.
The ability to think.
To reason.

This God was more than able
to handle all of my questions.
It's my peers who couldn't.
My church.

They would tell me it was ok to have the questions.
Just not in front of the children.
Not in front of the young adults.

Don't make them stumble.
Don't cause them to question.

So, my voice got stifled.
I quit speaking up.

I stopped going to bible studies.
Even though I was still studying.

No more prayer meetings.
Even though I was praying more than ever.

To a God who I still somehow believed in.

But, here's the deal...

Over the years I have met others.
People who aren't afraid to ask the questions.
Some who have walked the same road as I have.

Last year, I enrolled in Keith Gile's online *Square One Course*.
As I met new friends, I realized I was in a safe space.
I wasn't alone.

And after Keith heard my story?
The part about me feeling *silenced*?
He spoke right to my heart.

He said his hope would be
for me to find my voice again.
That I would see there are others
like me who I can speak to.
Write how I'm feeling,
and they will understand.
Maybe even learn from my story.

My voice is coming back.
It's slow, and a little afraid still.

My husband told me I should be "proud" of my writing.
I'm not there... yet.

But being truthful feels right.
Speaking up feels good.

And finding new friends along the way?
Let me just say...
I'm here for it.

PART VI

yellow

Ms. Shock, you're very yellow.
You always wear yellow.
If you were a color... you'd be yellow.

Ok. Well, in my defense...
it's one of our school colors.
More importantly,
it is the color of sunshine.

Oh, and I also had a teacher
walk by me this morning
and ask me why I am always smiling.

Sorry, not sorry.
Smiling is my favorite.

And yellow is too.

Isn't it funny how a person who
deals with anxiety/depression
can get accused of smiling too much?

Maybe there is just something more
inside of me that shines through
in spite of the hard days?

Maybe there is just something
inside of me that shines through
because of the hard days?

A thankfulness that is "other."

A gratefulness that bears witness
to something/someone greater than me.

And did I mention, I really like yellow?

s'up

How about one more yellow story?
From back in the day.
Another time I wore yellow.
Bright, sunny, yellow.
To a hipster church.

What was I thinking?
I guess…
Maybe,
I wasn't?

We had signed up to be greeters.
I'm a good greeter.
Hi!
Hello!
Good morning!

They may not let me preach,
but they will let me greet.

There we were.
It was one dreary, winter morning.
Kev and me.
Standing at the door.
Kevin… looking cool.
Me… looking yellow.

It was a nice thought.
Yellow goes good
with my blonde hair
and blue eyes.

I was ready.
These young college kids?
They needed some joy.
Joy on Sunday Morning.

Momma Shock...
Bringing the love.

That's what I thought, at least.
Until they started to roll in.

Did I mention we were old?
Second oldest couple in the church.

Hi there!
Good morning!
Welcome!
How's it going?
Great to see you!

Oops.
Why?
Why are they all so quiet?
What is that look they are giving me?
It almost looks like they want me to shut up.

Mind you, Kevin was doing great.
He wasn't wearing yellow.
He wore black.
He looks good in black.
He looked the part.

And when the college students walked in?
He would just nod his head at them.
S'up?
And they would nod back.

Oh wait… so the yellow thing?
The bright, sunshiny day thing?
We aren't doing that here?

Turns out?
No.
Not there.

I put my little yellow sweater back in the closet that day.
No place for yellow in a hipster church.
Something Paul said about *becoming all things to all people?*

The next Sunday?
I wore black.
S'up?

i'm not leaving the faith

I never have been.
It's actually the opposite.
You could say I am diving deeper.

My whole life I've been frolicking in the shallow.
Staying near the water's edge.
My eyes on the shore.

Horrified of what may be out there in those deep waters.
In just deep enough to have little waves rolling in over my ankles.
Maybe even up to my knees.

But definitely not too deep.
I needed to see what might be lurking in there.
Steering clear of those dang jellyfish.

Even worse?
Well, I mean... have you seen Jaws?

Then, about ten years ago,
I started to wade a little deeper.
Believing God was with me in this scary journey.
Big enough to protect me
and my precious little faith.

I began by backing into it all.
Eyes still on the shore,
While the waves crashed over me.
Nearly drowning.
So afraid.

Why am I doing this?
Maybe I should just go back to building my own little castle in the sand?

But, something was calling me.
Out.
Out into the vastness.

I realized it would be so much easier
if I would just turn around.
Take my eyes off the shore.
Face the fears.
Dive into those crashing waves.
Head on.

And then?
Just keep swimming.
Out into the deep.
The ever-expansive blue waters.

Asking questions.
Humbled by how naive I've been.

Yes, there are sharks lurking.
Scary creatures all around.
Maybe even a whale that could swallow me whole?

But the beauty is worth the price.
The freedom to explore.
The adventure of it all.

So, I ask the questions.
The really deep ones.
The crazy ones it seems no-one wants to ask.

Deeper and deeper I go.
Not looking back.
Believing there is more.
My faith expanding as I go.
And the best part?
There is a God whose love is deeper
than anything I could venture out into.

we're in this race together

You can read what I write,
but please don't follow me.

Let me explain...

I remember when we had
a pretty nasty church split back in the day.

We were broken.

The dreams we had about
leading a big college ministry
were shattered.

All at once,
they came crashing down.

We leaders looked right in the eyes of our students
and said,

Don't follow us - we don't know where we are going.

Somehow, though?
They did stay with us.

It just looked different, that's all.
It looked more like them walking alongside of us.

We shed so many tears.
And asked God "*Why?*" a whole lot.

Mistakes had been made by all parties involved.
Honestly, we were truly humbled by it all.

I'm not sure we have ever fully recovered.
We've moved on,
but now we walk with a limp.

You know what?
I think the limp is good.

Especially if we can admit we have one.
I am no longer trying to outrun anyone.

The race I'm on now?
Well, it's way more slow-paced.

Lots of resting.
Trusting.
Breathing.

Lots of stopping to look around.
Maybe even picking up
a seashell or two along the way.

Helping others when they fall down.
Meeting so many other runners.
Looking them in the eyes.
Helping them wipe their tears.

But...
I'm definitely not
telling anyone to follow me
anymore.

I'm done pretending I am the way.

Jesus is the way.

So, I will gladly tell you
to keep your eyes on him
as you walk/crawl/limp/rest
alongside of me.

This life might be short.
The race is long.

We need each other.
I know this now more than ever.

power

I used to think the power of the Holy Spirit
was about a certain kind of power.

Like a Superhero's power.
Strong.
Brave.

Able to go be a missionary in a scary place.
Standing up for Jesus.
Saying no to sin.
Not drinking, cussing, or gossiping.
And not hanging with those who do.

That kind of power.

So, here's what I'm learning.

There is a certain kind of power that is talked about in the Bible.
Paul talks about it in the book of Ephesians.
It's a different kind than what I thought.

It says that we, being rooted and established in love,
would have the power to grasp...
How deep and wide the love of God is.

A love that surpasses knowledge.

Ok.
Back it up.
Paul is praying for us to be strengthened by the Holy Spirit.

But for what?
Why do we need strength?
Strength for what?

What kind of power are we talking about?
The power is to know.
To know God's love.
To understand this love.

It must not be easy.
He is on his knees, praying we can get this.

Then it says if we do grasp it?
We will be filled to the measure of all the fullness of God.

So, this must be a big deal.
It must be more love
than we are able to comprehend.

The Holy Spirit has to strengthen us
in our inner being
to know this love.
Must be some kind of love.

Not the power to understand all the big doctrines.
Not the power to withstand temptation.
Not the power to stand up for Jesus.
Not in this verse.

This power is simply about *love*.
Except it doesn't sound so simple.

It sounds huge.
Eternal.

Everlasting.
And big enough for every single one of us.

I know, right?
Can't be that big.
That's too big.
That's too much.
That doesn't even make sense.

Exactly.
That is why, today, I'm praying for all of us
to have the supernatural power needed to understand.

I'm thinking...
All the other stuff
falls into place
when we know this love.

May we know this love.

a messy, muddy life

I had a dream.
Last night.

So real.
So memorable.
Need to write it down.

I was hanging out with my best friends.
Ready to take a hike in the woods.

It had just rained.
Inches and inches of rain.
A muddy mess.

I thought for sure we would cancel the hike.
Can you imagine walking in that?

But... as I looked in front of me.
My friends were taking off their shoes.
They were rolling up their pants.
Ready for the challenge.

Are you kidding me?
We're doing this?
We're really doing this?

Yep.

Let's go.
It's gonna get messy.
We are about to get dirty.
Real dirty.

There may be snakes and probably lots of bugs.
Mosquitos.
And I'm a magnet for mosquitos.

Dang it.
Ok.

Oh, and no men are with us.

Just us girls.

And there is a little laughter.
Some talk of grounding.
Turns out, going barefoot is good for you?

Well then.
Let's hike.

I woke up this morning
and I actually thought about
going on a hike today.

It would be muddy.
The rain was heavy last night.
I could take off my shoes.
Re-enact the dream.

Then I remembered.
In my dream?
I was not alone.

We were not alone.
We were all in it together.

I don't have to hike the woods,
barefoot and alone.

This dream seems to be significant.

Right now, in my life.
In all of our lives.

We women?
We are strong.
We can laugh at the days to come.
We can do hard things.

Together.
There is so much to be done.
Right here.

We were made for such a time as this.

Let's go.
Let's get dirty.

It will be hard, and gross, and scary,
Which is exactly what we were made for.

To love so deeply we are willing
to roll up our jeans and enter in.
Together.

I'm grateful for this day.

May we see what it means to go for it.
In the little and the big.
From the dirty diapers,
to taking care of elderly parents.

From our own backyards,
to the nations.

The mess makes life worth living.
Let's just make sure
we laugh along the way.

in the midnight hour

Dear Mom of littles,

I know.
I remember.
Long days.
Even longer nights.
Will I ever sleep again?
Am I going crazy?
I must be crazy.

Four kids.
What was I thinking?
They are cute, but...
It's agonizing sometimes.
Failure seems so real.

And why do people show up at my door only when my house is trashed?
Oh... maybe because it is messy more often than it isn't.
Toys and laundry and books and bottles.
Will it ever end?
How will I ever make it?

Listen.
You will.

They will have big feet soon.
I can't tell you the times I still look at my boys' feet and think...
How in the world?
Those were just chubby sweet little piggies,
and now they are man feet?
How?
Time moves fast, that's how.
Slow days.
Fast years.

Here's my little piece of advice.
Just for today.
Get down on their little level.
Make eye contact.
Look them in the eye.
Ask them what they need?
Love them where they are.

Look into their little eyes.
See past their behavior,
through to their need,
and bless their need.

I remember thinking I never had time with Jesus
because I never could get by myself.
But Jesus is in them.

So, I'm saying...
Look for Jesus in them.
I know, right?
Easier said than done.

Biggest thing?
Make good deposits.
Make so many good deposits that on the bad days?
In the bad moments?
They know you love them.

Their bank account is filled up with enough love from you that they can actually hear you.

This is meant to encourage you.
Deep breath.

Get down.
Someday soon
you will be looking up at them.
I'm not even joking.

I know, I know.
I used to hate it when people said, *don't blink.*

Shut up.
I wanna blink.
I wanna get through it
and know I made it without going crazy.

I'm here to tell ya.
You will.
And your kiddos will too.
All our shortcomings?

There is counseling for that.
I just know my kids will need counseling.
And they will be better for it.
I will accept whatever they decide
to tell that sweet therapist
who has to undo some of what I've done.

God bless them.
And God bless you.
And may God bless us all.

I'm going back to sleep now.

But... young momma?
You are on my heart and mind.
I'm praying for you and with you in this very midnight hour.

Hugs to all.

an open heart

What does that even mean?
How do I get one of those?
And what does it even look like to have one?

These are my thoughts of late.

And I'm thinking the opposite would be?
A closed heart.

Or, we could talk about...

A soft heart vs. a hard heart.
A warm heart vs. a cold heart.

All of these seem to work
with where my thoughts are taking me.

It's all about posture.
The posture of my heart.

If I am closed off?

Not honest with others?
With Myself?
With God?

My heart will begin to shrivel up.
Become hard and cold.

In this world we are living in?

It's so easy to go inward.
Become about self.
Protecting me.
Saving my own.

Praying for a "hedge of protection."
Looking out for me and mine.

Ya know?
Safety first.

After all, the Bible does say to
Guard your heart.

How do we do this?

Should I put my heart in a box?
Lock it up?

Make sure nothing can hurt me anymore.
No-one can hurt me.

Should I stop with the vulnerability?

Never let them see me sweat.
Or cry.
Or be sad.

I'm not anxious or depressed.
Nope.
Nothing to see here.

It's way better for me and you if I just shut up.
Quiet the face.

Play like everything is great.
And stay back.
Keep my distance.

No time for up close and personal.
Closeness just breeds heartbreak.

An open heart leads to a broken heart.

Putting my life out here on display.
Being willing to risk being known.
Willing to dive deep.
Not knowing when I can come up for air.

It's scary, I know.

But, without it?
When I'm in protection mode?
Something inside me dies.
The light dwindles.

How will I ever know I am really loved?
If I am not real.

If in fact, you love a fake version of me?
Is it really love?

I want to be known,
really known,
and loved.

With a "for real" kind of love.

And I want to be able to love you,
for who you are.

Not who you pretend to be.
Not the "first date" kind of infatuation.

But the "real life, nitty gritty,
been married for twenty-nine years" kind.

This is how God loves.

We see it in the person of Jesus.

He saw right through people,
looked right in their eyes,
straight through to their hearts.
He looked passed their outward behavior,
saw through to their need,
and then blessed their need.

We can do this too.
Bless each other.
If we are willing to open up to one another.

Don't get me wrong.
It isn't necessary for us
to share everything with everyone.

But how about taking some baby steps?

Let someone in.
Lean in.
Go there.
Trust our heart to another.

Maybe it starts with being real with God.
We can let the God who already knows, know.

May we feel the love that Jesus has for us.
May we open our hearts to him.
Let him soften them.

Maybe, just maybe,
The whole guarding of our hearts?

It's not keeping them hidden away.
Maybe it's actually keeping them out here.
In a place where we can see each other.

Alive and open.

Knowing and being known.

Because out of our hearts?
Comes the wellspring of life.

leave the light on

The light on... and the door open.
Words for young families to live by.

Kev and I got a whole lot of things wrong in our parenting years.
I can give you a list of what we would do differently if we could go back.

But one thing we did do right?
And one thing we want to pass onto our kids?

Well, we just have always had an open-door policy in our family.
Our children knew they could knock on our bedroom door
at any time... day or night.

If they were scared.
If they needed a hug.
If they had a question.

C'mon on in.

I read somewhere about the teenage years.
This is when your kids will want to talk.
In the late hours of night.

You are not kidding.
It is no joke.
11:00, 11:30, 12:00 a.m.
Here one of them comes.

Ugh.
I need to get up in the morning.
I'm so tired.

Really?
We couldn't have done this at 7:00?
Nope.
Right now.
Ok... (with a yawn, and a stretch, and a sigh).
We are doing this.

Honesty.
Fears.
Big questions about faith.
Small stories about friends.

And maybe even some stories that I would never want to hear.
Telling myself...
Don't look shocked
And
Pretend this doesn't surprise you.

Poker face.
Let the words come.
The tears flow.

Sleep comes later.
Listening now.

Ready to give grace.
Willing to be present.

Looking into their eyes.
No matter their age...
Three, five, ten, or twenty.

Parenting is being in it for long haul.
Not always having their laundry done,
or the perfect meal on the table.

But being available.
Enjoying their lives.
Walking through the dark times.
Leaving the light on.

grown up kids

Who would have thought?
Just yesterday they were in my arms.
Depending on me.

Little faces looking up at me while I rocked them.
Hours of rocking and singing.
Singing and rocking.
Who would fall asleep first?
Them or me?

Go to sleep, oh go to sleep, my little Lyssa.
Over and over.
Her eyes would get heavy,
her little head would get sweaty,
and she would relax into a deep sleep.
Beautiful little Lyss.
And it was the same for our other three.

I mean, the words changed...
My little Drewbie,
My little Layna,
My little Lancie.

Then?
I blinked.

We have adult children.
Four amazing grownups
with lives of their own.

Planning their futures.
Spouses and houses.

Grandkids have been made.
Life is flying by.

And I still get the same kind of feelings.
The ones I had while they were little.

Am I doing enough?
Do they know I care?
Are they alright right now?

Do they need to be rocked?
No, really.
Sometimes, I just wanna rock them.
Hold them tight and sing about my love for them.
Sing loud and rock hard.
Let them know how much Jesus loves them too.

But this is just not that season anymore.
It just isn't.

And I get confused.
What is my role?
How do I know?
Am I intruding?
Should I back off?

How do I do this "mom of grown-up kids" thing?
So much of the time, I feel so inadequate.
Lots of times I feel selfish.

Should I be working?
Maybe I shouldn't.
Maybe I should devote more time to their needs?

Stop typing and knit something, Karen.
But I don't knit.
So, there's that.

I should invite them over for supper tomorrow night.
Oh wait, I have cheerleading.

I'm tired from work.
You see, I have had it all backwards.
I stayed home with them for twenty years.
Now I'm working.
Out in the world loving on high school kids.
Writing a book.
Small group on Thursday.
I feel busy.
Should I stop it all?

So, I talk to my daughter.
Little Layna who is all grown up now.
A mature, beautiful, twenty-six old.
Married, with a dog.
Our grand-puppy.
I tell her my dilemma of not feeling like a good momma.
She says this is not true.

Do I embarrass you?
She says *no*.
You know, with all I say and do?
Again, the answer is *no*.
Not at all, in fact.
She tells me I'm ok.
You're our mom, Mom.
We love you and we know how much you love us.

She sweetly tells me to stay in my own lane.
My life looks different than any other momma's.
It always has.
Why?

Well, simply because all of our lives look different.
We all have different stories.
Different dreams.
Different pasts.
Different gifts.

I'm pretty sure this is something to celebrate.

Life is going by so fast.
My lane seems to be somehow speeding up.
Maybe I need to keep my eyes on the road ahead.
Stop looking around and comparing.

I've realized this along the way.
When I compare?
I either get really insecure or full of pride.
It doesn't do any good.

And in a world of social media?
We are comparing snapshots of our lives.
And I can easily get caught up in thinking I'm not enough.

Turns out, little Layna might be right.

My lane today, Lord.
Teach some kids.
Do some laundry.
Drink some coffee.

And this weekend?
I get to rock some grandbabies.

easy like sunday morning

I have to admit, Sundays have not been easy for most of my life. When I was little, I remember my dad coming in to wake me up for church.

Whoop-tee-do! Whoop-tee-do!
Time to get up and go to Sunday school!

While tickling me, of course.
Daaaad!!!! Stop it!
Moooommm!!! Tell Dad to leave me alone!

Mom would tell him to stop.
He would not.

I would be so mad.
Turns out, laughing while angry is actually a thing.

This was not a one-time event.
Every. Single. Sunday.
Even when I was in high school.

Sidenote ~ I miss that man.

Church was a hassle for me.
Dressing up.
Sitting there for an hour.

A whole hour.

Playing Tic Tac Toe
on the back of the attendance sheets.
Following along with the bulletin,
dreading the upcoming sermon part.

Oh, and then waiting around afterward
for Mom and Dad to quit *fellowshipping*.
Church was just kind of a pain when I was young.

Then there were some years
where Kev and I didn't go at all.
We thought about it a whole lot.
Just could never quite get enough energy up to go.
And I no longer had the tickle monster to motivate me.

At some point though, we jumped in.
All in.
Sunday mornings.
Sunday evenings.
Wednesday nights.
And any other time the church doors were open.

We became leaders.
Youth leaders.
College leaders.
Community group leaders.

Years and years of Sunday mornings.
And you will never guess
how I motivated our children to wake up.
It just seemed right.
And they hated it just like I used to.

I grew to love church.
The community.
The singing my heart out to God.
The message that would point me back to Jesus.

Our kids liked it too, for the most part.
We were literally the first ones there
and the last ones to leave.

For so many years, it was great.
Until it just wasn't anymore.

Things got all kinds of messed up.
I had questions about God.
And almost everyone wanted me to stop asking.
I was a leader.
Leaders don't have questions.

Shhhh....
Just have faith, Karen.
We can't know these things.
His ways are not our ways.
Believe what we tell ya.
Don't rock the boat.
And for Heaven's sake, don't scare the children.

I can honestly say,
I tried to shut my mouth.
I tried to be gentle and quiet.
Only ask my husband.
My poor husband.

It didn't work out so well.
I couldn't fake it on Sunday mornings any longer.
Or any other day of the week.

When Rob Bell came along
and wrote a book about these questions,

I came out into the open with all of mine.
Yes!
These are the same questions I have.

Shhhh...

Rob Bell is putting bad thoughts in your brain.
He is leading you astray.

Ummm...
Nope.
He definitely is not.
He is just putting words
on all of the thoughts I've had for years.

And I watched as the celebrity pastors shunned him.
Farewell, Rob Bell.
Like a tennis match,
my head turned back and forth.
He said this.
They said that.
He tweeted this.
She tweeted that.

Holy crap.
I better *Shhhh* some more.

And the more I kept my mouth shut?
The more I sank into depression.
I started having anxiety attacks on Saturday nights.
Kev would pray over me before we went to sleep.

After the service was over one Sunday morning,
I was standing with a group of my friends.

They were honestly helping me breathe.
The struggle was real.

The pastor's wife came over to our group and said,

Ladies, disperse... Get out of your little huddle and get over there and greet the new people.

Panic.

It was then that I realized
this wasn't so much about building God's Kingdom.
It was very much about building
this one little church's kingdom.

This was over ten years ago,
but it slaps me in the face every single time I think of it.

Don't get me wrong, I love Jesus.
I want to know Jesus more and more.
I want to love like he loved.
I want to serve like he served.
Pray like he prayed.

Even *lose my life* for his sake.
But no longer am I willing to *lose my life* for the sake of a man's kingdom.

No longer do I want to bow down
to a man or board of any kind.

After I wrote a blog about LGBTQ+?
I told Kevin I felt so free.
I had so much peace.
He smiled and admitted he was glad
there was no elder board for us to answer to.
Yep.
We actually do answer to someone.
To God.

And I feel really good about answering
to the God I have grown to know.

So, it's Sunday morning as I type.
An easy Sunday morning.

Pajamas still on.
Coffee in hand.
And a peace about it all.

It took me a few years to feel this peace.
To feel no guilt or shame about not being in a pew.

And now since the guilt is gone?
I am actually free to go if I want to.

This has been a long journey.
Years of panic and anxiety.
Meditations and medications.
Counselors telling me over and over
it was/is ok to take a break.

Kevin has made a Sunday morning playlist
for us to listen to in our Florida room.
We have had the best talks.
I still ask him the hard questions.
He still smiles and says "I have no idea."

We've grown closer together.
Slept in when we've felt like it.

Maybe listened to a podcast or sermon.
Or danced to some Lionel Richie.
All to the Glory of God.

Oh, and I am actually
heading to a church service this afternoon.
And we will go to our daughter's church next weekend.

I am no hater.
We are just ok where we are.
Jesus said his yoke is easy.
I'm just saying...
Easy like Sunday morning.

i can feel it in the air

The time of year when we said goodbye to both Dad and Mom.
Nine years apart.
Buried on the same day.
September twenty-sixth.
Certain songs remind me of their time in hospice.
Music playing as we sat by their beds.
Each of us got our own time alone with them.
Saying all the things we needed to say.

I told them I loved them so many times in those last days.
I held their hands.
I remember saying *Thank you*.
Reminding them of what amazing parents they were.

Staring at their frail little bodies.
Telling them they could go.
Just simply letting them know
we were all gonna be alright.

Head on over to the other side.

And you know what is crazy?

I got to hold both of their hands
as they took their lasts breaths.

I CAN FEEL IT IN THE AIR

What are the odds?

And as I think about it?
It seems like it was a gift from God.

Remember the dang rapture movie?
How terrified I was?
Sleeping in between my parents that night.
Holding both of their hands so tight.
And not just that night.
Lots of nights.
Staring at the ceiling in the dark,
not wanting them to go without me.

Do you see the gift?

As a forty-one and fifty year old daughter,
I had the honor
of holding each of their hands
as they went on without me.

I was ready.
Well, maybe not totally.
Are we ever ready to say good-bye?

But I actually got to watch both of them take their last breaths.
And usher both of them into the arms of Jesus.

God is so good to redeem those nights of fear and dread.
To walk with me through the valley of the shadow of death.

I have heard so many stories of God's goodness in times like this.
Where the veil becomes thin between here and there,
and we know we are sending our loved ones to a better place.

So, as this season rolls around again.
I will sit by our open windows
and watch the trees blow in the wind.

I will talk to my parents as if they can hear me.
And thank Jesus for being with us through it all.

team up

The best marriage advice I've ever gotten.
In the midst of a tragedy that had happened in our family,
Kevin and I were arguing over something small.
I was stunned that I/we could be so frivolous at a time when our world was crashing in.

When I texted my mentor about the whole situation,
I mentioned the fighting part.
She replied with the most beautiful, consoling words about what was happening.
And at the end of the text, she simply said...

Team up, you two need each other right now.

Ah... yes.
We are a team.
Team Shock.

I cannot tell you how much this helped in that moment.
It still helps today.
I often think of these words.
Kev and me.
A team.

I was listening to a podcast on how wrong we have gotten the male headship thing in Fundamentalist Christianity.
It was so eye opening.

In the circles we used to run in?
Male headship was talked about all of the time.

We had a pastor who lectured Kevin about needing to lead me better, blaming him for the issues I was having with my anxiety.
Can you imagine?

So, guess what this whole "man leads the woman" led to.
Me... trying to lead Kevin... to lead me.
Haha.
I laugh now, but it is so true.

I spent a whole lot of years trying to figure out how I could get Kevin to lead me and our family the way I thought he should lead.

When we decided we were a team?
That is when it turned around.
When I got off his case about quiet times and Bible reading?
Our marriage began to flourish.

Why?
Because I stopped trying to lead him to lead me.
I left him alone.

We realized that I have the capacity to lead in some areas just as much, if not more.
I have strengths and he has strengths.
I don't need to get to him to lead me in the things I'm strong in.

Yes, Kevin has so many gifts and so much wisdom.
But, so do I.

Our gifts may not line up with the typical male/female stereotypes.
And that is ok.
Nope.
Better than ok.
It's beautiful.

So, I no longer put the pressure on him
to be something I "think" he needs to be.
I no longer put the pressure on myself
to try to "get under his headship" when it comes to our marriage.

We think and act like a team now.
We function as a team.
We build our lives around our strengths.
We make decisions together.

I cheer him on.
He cheers me on.
We look for the good in each other.

This sounds like we have the perfect marriage.
Nope.
We still need to be reminded that we are a team.
A whole lot.

We are still learning how to win at this thing called marriage.
And I more than understand that some marriages don't work out.
I think I'm just trying to help take the pressure off.
We don't have to be something/someone we were not meant to be.

There is so much life to be lived.
Fun to be had.
Ice cream to be eaten.

Maybe?
Can we try teaming up with our partner?
Look at each other as equals who each have gifts to contribute?
Maybe even have our team meetings while we eat the ice cream?

So, for today.
Whoever is in our life, and in our house.
Let's team up.

grateful

Would I have loved for my anxiety
to be healed by a prayer?
Of course.
Who wouldn't have?
No one asks to have this kind of mental anguish and pain.

But...
Can we talk for a minute about my life in the midst of it?
Let me show you two lists:

Wait.
Before we start.
Hear me.
This is not bragging.
There is a point to all of this.

1.) *IN SPITE OF MY ANXIETY:*

> I have raised four children.
> I homeschooled all four.
> I have been a pretty fun wife.
> I am an even more fun grandma.
> Mom and Dad lived with us for 10 years.
> I had the honor of ushering both of them into Heaven.
> I have also had the honor of watching several of our little family members enter this world.

Kevin and I have led high school and college ministries.
We started **She Has A Name**.
I wake up in the morning and still praise God.
I have instructed baton twirlers.
I have coached cheerleaders.
I have been a substitute teacher.
Oh, and I have been writing a book.

2.) BECAUSE OF MY ANXIETY:

I pray... a whole lot... on my knees.
I sing a whole lot louder.
I love a whole lot deeper.
I hug a whole lot harder.
I see others.
I feel their pain.
I know their pain.
I get it when one of my cheerleaders struggles with it.
I appreciate the days when I don't have it.
I rejoice with others on days when they don't.
I'm not as judgmental.
I write.
I have a dog.
I eat better.
I exercise more.
I see a therapist.
I am practically a doctor.
Well, I mean...
My degree is from Dr. Google.
Does that count?
Oh, and I can laugh at myself.
I read books.
I meditate.
I memorize scripture.
I'm actually not as afraid of the big stuff.

I dance in our kitchen.
I dance with my husband.
I dance with our grandkids.
And I'm writing a book about it all.

Did I mention I take deep breaths?
I'm taking one as I type.

It can be scary to put myself out here like this.
But I want others to know.

I'm ok.
I'm actually better than ok.
I'm grateful for my crazy mind today.

full of delight

I had a counseling session the other day.
And at the very end of our time,
I was starting to stand up,
and gather my stuff.

My therapist looked me in the eye and said,
Karen, you are delightful.

What?
I know I looked confused.
Are you kidding me?
Delightful?
Full of delight?

I had just gotten done telling her all of my struggles.
We had just spent an hour together.

I cried most of time.
I was so tearful.
So full of tears.

I had just told her about all of my fears.
How fearful I am.
So full of fear.

I told her what I am dreading.
How dreadful I feel.
So full of dread.

I complained about how stressful my life can be.
So full of stress.

I also admitted to my arrogance and pride.
Prideful.
Yep... full of pride.

I told her about a certain scenario.
She spoke life into it.

I thanked her for her insight.
She is so insightful.

And then she said the word...
Delightful.

C'mon.
She could have used any of the words I just used.
Fearful, prideful, stressful.
Why delightful?

We have sat across from each other for a few years now.
Shouldn't she be sick of me?

Round and round and round.
Just when I think I'm over the struggle.
Here we are again.
It can feel so shameful.
How did we get back here?
She tells me how we are not back at the beginning.
We are still going forward.
Maybe we have hit a bump.

But I now have tools to help myself.
I just have to be reminded of those tools.
And reminded of my identity.

She reminds me gently.
I am not my fears.
I am not defined by my struggles.

And I shake my head.
Listening.
Ready to learn.
Re-learn.

Step back and see the big picture.
There is hope.
There is a peace to be had.

My jaw relaxes.
My shoulders drop.
I take a deep breath.

And she speaks life.
Tells me I am *delightful*.

I just looked up the word.
It means pleasant, enjoyable, attractive.
Really?

Ok.
I will take it.
I will lean into it.

In the midst of my anxious little life.
There is room for delight.

Even as I type this?
I'm afraid you might think I'm *prideful*.

This is all so hard for me to say.
Telling the whole world I see a therapist.

I still struggle.
I could pretend I don't.

But, would that be helpful?
Full of help?

I'm thinking instead?
It just might help someone else to hear all of this.

Your fears and anxieties don't define you.
Telling another person/counselor about them
might be just what you need.
You don't have to tell the whole world like I do.

But there is rest in knowing we are not alone in all of this.
And in speaking the truth to each other.

The words I hear in my head about who I am?

They are powerful.
Dare I say it?
Full of power.
I need some life spoken into this delightful little head of mine.
You do too.
And it starts with being honest about the lies you hear.
Let's be honest.
Let's speak some life into each other today.
May our mouths be full of life.

there's no ending, karen

Aunt Norma said this to me back in the day.
She was singing a song and forgot how it ended.
I have it all on video.
She was the cutest.
She kept dancing while she said it.

And these sweet words keep running through my mind.
Trying to end this book.
Finding the perfect way to close it out.

How?
How do I end something I am still right in the middle of?
All of the questions.
All the anxiety.
The counseling.
The learning.
The growing.

What is written in this book...
The thoughts I've had...
Any conclusions I've come to in this season...
They are all still evolving.
I have not arrived.

Even as I go back and read these poems,
I just keep wanting to expound on them.
Write more.
Say more ideas I've had since I wrote them.

I guess it is just the way this all works.

This book is a snapshot.
There is no big red bow to tie it all up.

It's more about the journey than the destination.
At least that's what I am learning.

You learn something new every day.

So, I will turn this manuscript in.
And have a certain peace in doing it.

A certain peace about my uncertainty.
Certainly uncertain.

Our faith shifts.
Our views change.

And you, taking the time to read this book?
To feel seen,
or even just trying to understand.

Thank you.

Our stories aren't over.
I will write on.

We will walk on.
Believing there are new mercies every morning.
Taking deep breaths.
Speaking life to each other.
Reminding each other.

We are never too much.
And we are always enough.

THANKS

Alyssa — Your life is a gift. I'm forever grateful I get to be your mom.

Andrew — You'll never know how much life, fun and adventure you bring to our lives. You'll never, never, never know.

Alayna — My little missionary. I'm so glad you have offered take care of me some day. Does Jake know?

Alanson — My baby. Your name means "happy one." Your smile says it all.

KG, Jake, and Hannah — Thank you for helping complete our little Shock family. You are the answers to this momma's prayers.

Kessa, Liv, Alice, and Axel J. — My dancing buddies. No one can bring tears to my eyes, and joy to my heart more than you. You make being a grandma so much fun.

Christen and Amy — These pages are filled with stories of our lives together. Thank you for walking through this messy, muddy life with me.

Leslie — You were the first person to encourage me to put my writings in a book. I remember where we were sitting when you said it.

Jaiden — Thank you for your constant reminders that it is all gonna be ok.

Keith — Thank you for believing in me and for giving me my voice back.

Matthew — Thank you for making this book publishing thing fun. You make it look easy. Have I told you lately how awesome you are?

My Square Three Family — Thank you for allowing me to be real. And for loving me so well.

Justin and Lisa — Thank you for being the very best neighbors. And for helping me see my writing is worth investing in.

Abbey — You call it poetry. You say I'm a poet. Thank you.

My Snider Kids — I wouldn't be doing this if it weren't for you. You all make me brave.

To my Facebook friends who have commented, messaged, and encouraged me to keep putting my stuff out there for the world to see. Thank you. You have no idea how much it all means.

For more information about Karen Shock,
or to contact her for speaking engagements,
please visit karenruthshock.com.

QUOIR

Many Voices. One Message.

www.quoir.com

Made in the USA
Las Vegas, NV
06 July 2023

74293696R10148